POLITICS IN THE GILDED AGE

NEW PERSPECTIVES IN AMERICAN HISTORY

UNDER THE EDITORSHIP OF JAMES P. SHENTON

GERALD SORIN, ABOLITIONISM:
A NEW PERSPECTIVE

Politics in
the Gilded Age
A New Perspective on Reform

John M. Dobson

FOREWORD BY JAMES P. SHENTON

PRAEGER PUBLISHERS
New York • Washington • London

PRAEGER PUBLISHERS
111 Fourth Avenue, New York, N.Y. 10003, U.S.A.
5, Cromwell Place, London SW7 2JL, England

Published in the United States of America in 1972
by Praeger Publishers, Inc.

Library of Congress Catalog Card Number: 78–170467

Printed in the United States of America

For Cindy: a ship of her own

Contents

Foreword

by James P. Shenton

Nothing in history is fixed in its interpretation. The historian is forever re-examining evidence or examining new evidence to develop new understandings of past events. As his awareness of the complexity of the human condition and of its social expression deepens, the historian struggles to incorporate these added dimensions within his discipline.

The process of historical reinterpretation, which adds excitement to the task of being a historian, in some measure is a reflection of the changing needs and interests of new generations. More fundamentally, new interpretations of history reflect the profound forces that operate to bring about social change. For the historian, like any other man, is not immune to the influence of the currents that shape the experience and attitudes of his time.

In the decades since the end of World War II, historians have increasingly employed the tools and techniques of analysis developed by sociologists, political scientists, social psychologists, and anthropologists. Armed with these interdisciplinary methods, they have been better equipped to probe the complex motivations of men. Their ability to analyze the extraordinary variety of mass behavior has been vastly improved by the use of statistical analysis and computers to unravel the meaning of mountains of raw data. It now seems possible to explain not only the behavior of a handful of people but that of whole cities, classes, and even societies.

More important than the changes in methodology are the changes in historians' attitudes and approaches, reflecting the

impact of vast social changes. Thus, for example, the black revolution in America and abroad has obliged historians to abandon
their traditional preoccupation with governing elites to examine
the interaction of whites and blacks on all levels of human experience. Americans have suddenly become aware that a vast segment
of their national life, that of nonwhites, has been shrouded in
neglect. And, because so much of the nonwhite experience has
been that of a downtrodden and oppressed people, historians have
had to begin to develop techniques of analysis that will permit an
understanding of how the common man functioned. In a world
growing smaller, a world in which the masses of mankind aspire
to a fuller dignity, historians are faced with the demand that they
probe the history of the many rather than the few. To meet this
demand, they are beginning to explore not only the history of nonwhites but also that of the neglected female. Similarly, historians
are beginning to look into the ways in which ethnic origin has
affected American whites—for example, the attitudes and behavior
of American labor.

The authors of this series, well aware of these significant
changes in the world and in historians' ways of interpreting it, are
attempting a twofold task. They seek, first, to synthesize the most
recent scholarship on a significant period or theme in American
history. Second, they attempt to project contemporary relevance
into past experience so as to give the student a fresh perspective
on material that may be familiar to him in more conventional presentation. The consistent emphasis on changing interpretations,
it is hoped, will stimulate interest in history as a dynamic discipline and will dispel any lingering vestiges of the myth that
historians are somehow above the fray, uniquely capable of pure
objectivity.

With the new effort to understand the individual in mass society
has come a desire to know more about the functioning of the
institutions that affect everyman. The family, the school, the system of criminal justice, the institutions of government, to name
but a few, are being subjected to deepening scrutiny by historians
as well as other social scientists.

In this book, Professor Dobson re-examines the political parties
of the Gilded Age. As he rightly notes, the parties of today are

not significantly different in structure, in methods of functioning, or in the pressures toward reform to which they are subjected. As in the nineteenth century, many observers today question whether the party system has relevance to contemporary democratic society. Why the challenge issued by the reformers of the Gilded Age failed is the focus of Professor Dobson's investigation.

It is dangerous to assume that the past is an infallible guide to the present, but a careful analysis of past experience can provide at least a basis for comparison between past and present. Whatever the inadequacies of the party structure of the Gilded Age, it did provide the political machinery that the United States required in the years after the Civil War. But the nation has undergone enormous changes since then. One wonders whether the party structure has changed too little—or too much—for today's needs. Professor Dobson's provocative study of the formative stages of the modern party system provides a new perspective on this contemporary dilemma.

Preface

In the period known as the Gilded Age, from the end of the Civil War to the beginning of the twentieth century, American political parties became highly organized. In each of the two major parties, an elaborate structure developed, involving the establishment of local, regional, and national organizations intent upon winning and consolidating political power. As politicians succeeded in using this structure to increase and expand their influence, some citizens began to feel that the operations of party organizations were antithetical to good government and unresponsive to the wishes of the people. This group of concerned citizens called for changes—specifically, for reform of the civil service—which they felt would ensure honest, benevolent, and truly democratic government policies.

Consequently, this book tells a two-part story. The first part concerns the development and character of highly organized parties. The second describes the efforts of a group of dissidents who hoped, through the instrumentality of civil-service reform, to reverse the trend toward organization in the parties. The clash between the opposing forces peaked in the early 1880's, with the Presidential election of 1884 serving as a crucial test of which side would ultimately triumph.

The developments described in the following pages have profound relevance to our own times. Those Americans who, alarmed by political developments of the last few years, have pursued alternatives have counterparts in the group of disillusioned citizens who, a century ago, tried to alter political trends. In a very real sense, the early advocates of reform were locked in a struggle with the "establishment" of their day, represented, in this case, by party organizations that the reformers felt were ignoring the needs and wishes of the people as a whole. The rise, fleeting success, and eventual disintegration of their movement have lessons for anyone interested in working to make government more relevant and responsive. The reader must decide for himself whether their experience should serve as a model to be emulated or as an example of what should be avoided in present-day confrontations.

Acknowledgments

Although it would be impossible to give individual credit to everyone who helped with this book, several deserve special mention. The first is Robert V. Bruce, whose enthusiasm, insight, and wit encouraged me to study the Gilded Age. No less significant is my debt to Richard N. Current, who guided me through the initial stages of this project, and to Walter Rundell, Jr., who encouraged me to complete it. I am also deeply grateful to James P. Shenton, editor of this series, and to Gladys Topkis and the staff of Praeger Publishers. The staffs of the Wisconsin State Historical Society and of the Stanford University libraries supplied me with sources, work space, and indulgence. Finally, I would like to acknowledge the assistance and support of three groups at Iowa State University: my colleagues in the department of history, the library staff, and the Sciences and Humanities Research Institute, which gave me a grant for the completion of this project.

PART I

The Development of Party Organizations

1. The Origins and Structures
of the Major Parties

How are you goin' to interest our young men in their country if you have no offices to give them when they work for their party?

—GEORGE WASHINGTON PLUNKITT, quoted in William L. Riordon, *Plunkitt of Tammany Hall* (1905)

In 1888, a member of the British Parliament named James Bryce produced one of the most thorough treatises ever written on the American political system. Although his own efforts were admirable, Bryce commented on the difficulty of studying American political parties: they lacked any legal basis. The Constitution, which provides the political historian with an outline for discussing the federal government, does not mention parties. With the exception of a cursory reference in the *Federalist Papers*, published just after the Constitutional Convention, the Founding Fathers said little publicly about political parties. Unanimously elected the nation's first President, George Washington appointed to his cabinet some of the most brilliant and talented citizens of the new republic, ignoring conflicts in their political attitudes and with each other. Yet these conflicts soon created a sharp division between those who favored more centralized federal power and those who emphasized local rights. But the Federalists did not become a party as such until they had, in the Hegelian sense, created their antithesis in the form of the Anti-Federalists, later to evolve into the Jeffersonian Republicans. The first two parties, then, came into existence almost simultaneously, and they persisted through the War of 1812.

After the war, in the so-called Era of Good Feelings, when most major political issues appeared to be resolved, Jefferson's Republican successors encountered little or no partisan opposition. In 1824, however, the single party's congressional caucus overlooked more popular men to nominate President Monroe's secretary of the treasury, William Crawford, for the Presidency. A native of Virginia who had migrated to Georgia, Crawford seemed to many of his opponents just another member of the Southern-oriented Virginia dynasty, which had already contributed four presidents. Northeasterners and Westerners wanted a national leadership that would reflect their own aspirations and attitudes. They, therefore, rejected the choice of the congressional caucus, and the one-party consensus was shattered. Among several others, Tennessee war hero Andrew Jackson and Massachusetts aristocrat John Quincy Adams were nominated by their respective state legislatures and proved to be the leading vote-getters in the election. But neither had the required majority of the electoral vote; so, by constitutional prescription, the decision fell to the House of Representatives. After a good deal of internal politicking, that body gave Adams the Presidency, at the same time creating the basis for a revival of the two-party system.

One of Crawford's initial supporters was Martin Van Buren, who had been schooled in the internecine New York State political wars and had inherited control of Aaron Burr's political machine. When Crawford failed to win the necessary votes, Van Buren shifted his allegiance to Jackson. Disappointed by the 1824 results, he used his skill and intelligence to build a powerful organization for Andrew Jackson's successful 1828 campaign. Four years later, in 1832, this organization called its first national nominating convention, symbolizing the birth of what eventually became the Democratic party.

Jackson's policies as President, including his opposition to the Bank of the United States and certain internal improvements schemes, encouraged his critics to form the rival Whig party. The Whigs had trouble creating a popular national platform in the face of the localism that characterized the prevailing political interests. So, in 1836 they ran three regional candidates for the Presidency, losing to Jackson's handpicked successor, Van Buren. Only the major depression that set in after 1837 gave the Whigs an issue on which they could defeat the Jacksonian Democrats. Unfortunately, their candidate, William H. Harrison, died almost immediately after being inaugurated, and his Vice-President, John Tyler, lacked the respect of the other Whig leaders. Attempting to build a new political coalition loyal to himself, Tyler raised the expansionist issue, which helped Democrat James K. Polk to seize power in 1844.

By the 1830's the antislavery impulse and its proslavery counterpart in the South were well on the way toward splitting the nation. In 1848 the Free Soil party was formed by idealistic and zealous abolitionists along with other Northerners disturbed by economic and political trends. After barely electing Zachary Taylor that year, the Whig party began to collapse. It had never been able to generate the traditions, ties, and leaders that had held the Democratic party together and enabled it to dominate the federal government in the 1850's. Some Whigs retreated into the Democratic party, particularly in the South, and others drifted into the anti-immigration American or Know-Nothing party. Those who considered the extension or continuance of slavery incompatible with their moral principles or detrimental to their economic ambitions joined forces in the infant Republican party. Once the Republican coalition had broadened its platform and drawn in many of the Know-Nothings, it assumed the role of primary opposition to the Democratic party.

The smoldering sectional crisis burst into flame with the election of Republican Abraham Lincoln to the Presidency in 1860. By then, the diverse attitudes of the young party's adherents had coalesced into a forward-looking platform, which proved to be very popular in the North. Southerners read only far enough to determine that the platform included a plank opposing the extension of slavery into the territories. Proslavery forces throughout the South, threatened by this free-soil stand, decided that, if they failed to repudiate Lincoln and his platform, they would be admitting implicitly that the "peculiar institution" was immoral and should be eradicated. Led by South Carolina, the most insistent defender of Southern rights and traditions, eleven slave states seceded from the Union, thus removing themselves from the jurisdiction of the "Black Republican" President-elect. The disintegration of the Union, not slavery or abolitionism, suddenly became the major political concern of the day.

Throughout the ensuing war years, the Republican President tried to keep his administration as nonpartisan as possible. The culmination of Lincoln's efforts came in 1864, when he won re-election on a Union party ticket with a Democratic Vice-Presidential candidate, Andrew Johnson. Because of his deliberately neutral course, the President had constantly to justify himself to the Radical Republicans, who included some of the most idealistic as well as the most ambitious members of the Republican coalition. Their extremism, like that of dedicated abolitionists thirty years earlier, did little to reduce sectional frictions.

Whereas many Americans might have accepted Lincoln's lenient Reconstruction proposals, the Radicals violently objected to them. Even before the 1864 election, they had countered Lincoln's conciliatory program with the Wade-Davis Manifesto, a harsh plan for controlling the return of the seceded states to the Union. Lincoln failed to present his anticipated compromise proposal before his tragic assassination, and the responsibility for dealing with the Reconstruction crisis fell to Andrew Johnson, who proved singularly incapable of coping with it. The Radicals, who had armed for a conflict with a strong, wily, and respected President, completely overwhelmed his weak, clumsy, and unpopular successor. The utter destruction of Johnson's power as President thus resulted directly from the strength of Lincoln's administration.

The struggle between congressional Radicals and President Johnson helped to strengthen the foundations for the political parties of the future. The Union party coalition fell apart once its sole cohesive force, Lincoln, had disappeared from the scene.

Republican spokesmen claimed full credit for their party in bringing about a Union victory. Therefore, most of the political elements that had fought for restoration of the Union gravitated toward the powerful, Radical-dominated Republican party. Ex-Union soldiers, abolitionists, industrialists, war profiteers, and anyone else whose ambitions were furthered by the Northern success lined up under the Republican banner. The Radicals' clever handling of the Union issue assured them widespread support in the loyal states and enabled them to consolidate their power at the national level.

First the Radicals refused to seat representatives from the Southern governments that President Johnson's policies had called into being. Then they reinforced their control of Congress with victories in the elections of 1866. This control enabled them to deal with the South as they chose. The Radical Reconstruction program involved the establishment in the conquered states of governments that the Republicans could manipulate. In a gesture that blended idealism and practical politics, the Radicals pushed through three constitutional amendments, the last of which enfranchised the ex-slaves, who would steadfastly vote Republican. Finally, they impeached President Johnson, a totally unnecessary act since the Radicals already controlled both houses of Congress so effectively that they could easily override any Presidential veto. Having rendered the President completely powerless, they nevertheless wished to unseat him as well. But cooler heads prevailed in the Senate, and Johnson escaped removal. In 1868, Republican leaders enticed General Ulysses Grant away from his Democratic leanings and elected him President (a process the party repeated in 1952 with another popular general Dwight D. Eisenhower). During Grant's two terms, professional politicians had their way with the President, and both parties achieved a high degree of stability.

The strength of the Republican party lay in a galaxy of clever and provocative leaders, including Charles Sumner, Thaddeus Stevens, Benjamin Butler, and Roscoe Conkling. These expert politicians exploited the prevailing Union sentiment in their home districts to ensure their continued re-election to influential offices. They "waved the Bloody Shirt" until it became a ragged bundle of threads. Veterans' organizations such as the Grand Army of the Republic often served as little more than Republican party auxiliaries. During the war, Republican leaders had pushed several precedent-setting programs through Congress, including the Homestead Act, transcontinental railroad land grants, two national banking acts, and other elements of what Charles Beard has called the Second American Revolution. Consequently, party spokesmen could appeal to landless farmers, commercial entrepreneurs, and railroad speculators, among other groups. In the South, Republicans organized Union League Clubs, thinly disguised propaganda organizations that taught the blacks about the political rights the Radicals had championed for them. The freedmen, in turn, became stanch party supporters. Nationwide, the Republican party collected support from a diversified group of interests, many of them drawn by the party's proud claim that it had preserved the Union.

Dismayed by the increasing Republican domination, the disfranchised Southerners and the never-say-die Northern Democrats gathered together into a generalized opposition party. Any disgruntled person or faction could find shelter under the large, if somewhat leaky, Democratic roof. Nevertheless, the Democratic party often seemed close to collapse. Divided in 1860 and discredited in 1864, when they had predicted that a Lincoln victory would prolong the war another thirty years, Democratic leaders barely managed to keep the party alive. Lacking the Republican party's national appeal to Unionist sentiment, the Democrats had to depend quite heavily on local issues. This guaranteed them a degree of resiliency, for local interest groups continued to exist, whatever the party might suffer at the national or state level. For example, a good many white Southerners bitterly hated both white Republicans and enfranchised blacks and, therefore, supported the Democratic party as the only significant opposition to the Radical Reconstruction governments. Northerners with Southern sympathies, called Copperheads and traitors during the war, now emerged with strong followings in the lower tier of the Northern states. Some of the earlier Democratic machines had survived the war and revived stronger than ever, so that gradually a new national Democratic party emerged.

The two political parties that grew out of the Civil War shared the goal of obtaining political, economic, and social power and the perception that achievement of this goal required their own preservation. As the health of the party organizations became the most pressing concern of party leaders, they paid correspondingly less attention to such matters as putting forward well-qualified candidates and developing thoughtful platforms. The Republican party remained strong through its control of the federal government, with all the benefits and emoluments that accompanied that control, and through its impregnable regional and state organizations. The Democratic party subsisted on ambition, hatred of the Radical Republicans, and the cultivation of support among ex-Confederates in the South and urban laborers and immigrants in the North. As the two parties fought for control, each developed an elaborate structure, which ultimately proved to be a stabilizing influence on political behavior.

The two party organizations became quite similar over the years in part because the openness of the American political system allowed one party to copy the other's successful techniques. Also, both parties wished to present candidates for the welter of offices at every level of government, and politicians created party structures that mirrored these levels and offices. At the top, national committees and conventions met to select Presidential candidates. Below, state, county, city, and village or precinct organizations designated party candidates for offices at each level or selected delegates to regional conventions called for that purpose. In fact, American political party operations have not basically changed since the late nineteenth century, and much of what is described here applies as well to current party operations.

In the Gilded Age, a major political party depended for long-term sustenance upon the loyalty and voluntary work of a vast number of self-appointed partisans. The so-called primary caucus operated at the lowest political level, usually serving a ward or precinct in a city or a village or county. It consisted of a group of interested men with similar political goals who would gather to nominate candidates for local offices and to select delegates to the party organization at the next higher level, usually a regional convention. The process of nominating candidates for office and selecting delegates for higher-level conventions continued up the line until it peaked at a national convention.

Elections for local offices occurred far more frequently than the quadrennial Presidential races. James Bryce studied local conditions and discovered that the average voter in the state of Ohio had to elect some twenty or more officials every year. States differed in governing structure, but the case of Illinois illustrates the divisions found throughout the nation. Along with Presidential electors, every four years the state's voters elected a governor, a lieutenant governor, and several other state executive officers. It should be noted that Illinois had an unusually long gubernatorial term; governors served only one year in Massachusetts, and two-year terms were common elsewhere. The Illinois state treasurer held his office for two years, however, and was forbidden to succeed himself. The state's judicial system was elected as well, with supreme court justices elected to nine-year terms and circuit court judges to six-year terms. The state's legislative branch included senators, half of them elected every other year to four-year terms, while all state representatives were elected every two years. County officials served for four years, those in cities for two. Town officials had to be re-elected every year. The elections were spread throughout the year; federal, state, and county officers were elected in November, township and city leaders in April, and judges in June.

With a few local exceptions involving nonpartisan or uncontested races, each of these elections required the calling together of a primary or convention to nominate candidates. An individual voter would help to select officers in a variety of overlapping districts. In Illinois these might include a township, a city, and a county, as well as separately plotted circuit court, congressional, and general assembly districts. These divisions of government encouraged the development of a vast and intricate party mechanism. Many a man found full-time employment in local politics preparing for the next election, rarely more than a year away. Regardless of how lofty a position he had won, no politician could neglect local issues. A member of the House of Representatives in Washington had to remain in constant touch with his constituents at home because he was subject to recall every two years. Senators, despite their longer terms, were often even more ensnared in local politics, for the retention of their positions depended upon their controlling the state legislatures, which in those days chose the state's delegation to the United States Senate.

Inevitably, then, party leaders and activists tried to bring order out of this chaos by establishing lines of communication and control. Most aspirants for political offices joined local clubs. Theodore Roosevelt, for example, became a member of the Twenty-first Assembly District Republican Association in New York City, but only after obtaining sponsorship from some of the men who were already members. The club in turn nominated Roosevelt for a seat in the state assembly and helped to elect him. As many observers have noted, Americans enjoy forming clubs and organizations, and politicians naturally adapted these groupings to their own purposes. Every precinct and village had its Republican and Democratic clubs. Particularly in districts with high population concentrations, broad and influential political establishments flourished. Not every such organization was a machine, but every successful machine consisted of a soundly structured federation of local political organizations.

The classic example of the urban machine was the unit of the Democratic party of New York City, with its headquarters at Tammany Hall. The Tammany leaders were attempting to simplify and streamline the processes of candidate selection and election victory. At the same time, they frequently availed themselves of the many opportunities for personal enrichment. The Tammany machine was an amalgam of smaller groups. At the bottom, a precinct captain, frequently in the cozy atmosphere of his own saloon, would gather around him a band of loyal followers or ward heelers. The minor politico would then bargain the support of his group for candidates in higher level caucuses or conventions in exchange for patronage or other rewards. At the top of the machine stood the boss and his lieutenants, overseeing party operations throughout the city as well as deciding which trusted underlings to move into positions of prominence. To ensure voter loyalty, the machine provided a number of social services to its constituents, ranging from small financial gifts, through a speeded-up immigration or naturalization process, all the way to an important city or party job for a family member. The machine tried to control all city offices, executive, judicial, and legislative, so that it could guarantee police protection, immunity from prosecution, or a rigged judicial decision—for a price. In turn, the organization made its money by getting kickbacks from government workers' salaries or by selling franchises and building contracts to the highest bidder and collecting a rebate. The success and power of the Tammany Hall organization angered the two major rival Democratic groupings in the city: Irving Hall, which aspired to supplant Tammany as the chief beneficiary of machine-induced prosperity, and the County Democracy, a reform organization ostensibly determined to destroy Tammany and the abuses of self-seeking machines generally. Other elements of the Democratic party played upon immigrant and worker discontent and established powerful machines in Buffalo, Boston, Pittsburgh, and other cities. This sort of urban machine has survived in a few localities, the most outstanding example being Mayor Richard Daley's apparently unbeatable Democratic organization in Chicago.

While the Democrats controlled enclaves in Pennsylvania, Republican leaders generally ran that state. Senator Simon Cameron had built his organization into a strong force by the end of the Civil War. He was able to influence President Grant, late in his second term, to appoint the Senator's son, James Donald Cameron, to be secretary of war. When Grant's successor, Rutherford B. Hayes, failed to reappoint the younger Cameron, his father resigned from the Senate and had the state legislature send Don to Washington instead. From that time until the end of the century, Don Cameron and his father's able henchman, Senator Matthew S. Quay, dominated Pennsylvania politics. Perpetuation of the Cameron system did not depend upon petty bribery or protection payments. Rather, the machine simply saw to it that state and local authorities did not interfere with the operations of businessmen, honest and dishonest, and they, in turn, helped to drum up large majorities for the machine's candidates. Meanwhile, the bosses encouraged the growth of Pennsylvania industry in every way imaginable. The state's Republican delegates in Congress unremittingly advocated higher tariffs. Locally, the machine judiciously awarded state franchises to responsible contractors who would support the party. State police were always available to help out a strike-bound industrialist. Cameron and Quay obtained shares at low prices whenever a promising new corporation obtained a charter. These purchases ensured ample financial support for the bosses and state protection for the capitalists. Quay remained a powerful Senate boss until his death in 1904.

Relatively relaxed one-party regimes developed in the rural South and the Midwest, where elective positions were fewer and the amount of money involved far less than in urban areas, although here and there a county might fall under the control of unscrupulous supervisors or judges bent on making their positions pay very well. Hereditary or traditional preferences often made the politician's job quite simple. In Senator William B Allison's Iowa, the regular Republican nominee to any local or state position almost always won election; the Republican nominating conventions, rather than the bipartisan elections, were the major arenas for political struggles. In New Hampshire, where the Democrats virtually abandoned the field, contending interests aligned with opposing factions inside the Republican party. By the late 1880's, two competing railroads in the state, the Concord and the Boston & Maine, were engaging in economic rivalry which inevitably spread to politics. Although Republican Senator William E. Chandler's Boston & Maine support enabled him to retain his position until the turn of the century, advocates of the Concord Railroad sparred for positions and power within the Republican party organization.

The reconstructed South presented other examples of one-party rule. After 1877, the Democrats remained dominant in the South even through the Populist rebellion of the late 1880's and early 1890's. Consequently, the major political struggles took place among Democratic contenders at the nominating conventions. Interestingly enough, the philosophical differences dividing Southern Democrats closely resembled those that split

Northern politicians into two separate parties. In the North, the Republicans emphasized programs they thought would encourage industrialism, while the Democrats claimed to speak for the workers and farmers. But two Democratic senators from the same Southern state might well represent different economic and social viewpoints. For example, North Carolinians sent agrarian-minded Zebulon Vance to the Senate along with Matt Ransom, who favored industrial development. In Alabama's Senate delegation, John T. Morgan represented the old-line conservatives and James Pugh encouraged the state's growing steel industry. The concept of a solid Democratic South concealed competing attitudes under an acceptable party designation. Although recent efforts on the part of conservative Republicans may succeed in altering traditional practices, Southern politicians with a diversity of views continue to contend for a Democratic nomination. That nomination in Mississippi, for instance, still guarantees victory on election day.

States with prosperous machines representing both parties were something of an exception in the Gilded Age. At one extreme lay Indiana, whose Democratic party had remained strong throughout the war, particularly in the southern half of the state. Part of this strength derived from adverse reactions to the ultra-Unionist Republican governor and later Senator, Oliver P. Morton. His Radical leanings tended to alienate many who might otherwise have followed the Union party path out of the Democratic lineup. After the war, Indiana was one of the first Northern states to re-elect a Democratic governor, Thomas A. Hendricks. From then on, Indiana remained a swing state. Ohio shared many of Indiana's geographic and political characteristics along with a growing urban labor population, which tended to encourage the Democrats. The Republican party nominated two of Ohio's governors for President, Rutherford B. Hayes and James A. Garfield, precisely to attract wavering voters in the Buckeye State.

New York, Connecticut, and, less so, Massachusetts were doubtful for other reasons. In the urban, industrialized areas of all three states, the Democrats held sway because of their cultivation of workingmen's loyalty. In addition, certain conservative businessmen and free-traders, loosely referred to as Bourbons, gave monetary backing to the party. The rural areas were predominantly Republican, as were many of the big businessmen and industrialists, reflecting a trend common throughout the North (and one that persists today). The balance between urban and rural elements constantly shifted for a variety of reasons, not the least of which were economic influences. The industrial depressions and recessions of the period hit these three Northeastern states hard, and the citizens tended to blame the incumbent party. Therefore, these states experienced frequent changes in administration, as the less committed voters swung back and forth. In addition, a large proportion of the voters in New York, Connecticut, and Massachusetts considered themselves independents, making political certainty impossible. Both parties could maintain solid positions in the same state merely by controlling different parts of the government.

Although the winning of offices at every level was the primary goal of the parties, the methods employed varied widely depending upon local conditions. A boss who had worked his way up from the bottom often understood the operations of the local and regional organizations and was able to take advantage of weaknesses and opportunities along the way; indeed, the more intimately he understood local politics, the more likely he was to remain a political power. Democrat Arthur Pue Gorman, having begun his political career as a Senate page, moved up rapidly in Maryland politics. After he had served in the legislature at Annapolis, Gorman's Democratic friends made him president of the state-supported Chesapeake & Ohio Canal Company. His experiences as a local party leader and dispenser of patronage on the canal helped make Gorman a popular United States Senator by the 1880's. Such nationally prominent statesmen as Henry Cabot Lodge and Theodore Roosevelt also cut their teeth at the state-legislature level and never forgot their training in local politics.

Although the costs of campaigning in those days in no way matched those facing a political aspirant today, an independently wealthy man had a significant advantage over the less well-to-do. A few bosses bought in at the top, as did Zachariah Chandler, a millionaire businessman and merchant from Detroit. Chandler's success and contacts earned him a leading place in the city's society, which he used in his pursuit of political advancement, and his money assured him a means of financing his campaigns. By the time of the Civil War, Chandler had become an influential Republican senator. Choosing to side with the Senate Radicals, he retained his control of Michigan politics into the 1870's. A number of other wealthy men entered politics during this period, including Phileteus Sawyer, a Wisconsin millionaire lumberman, and Nelson Aldrich, a Rhode Islander later associated with the Rockefeller family. In the 1890's, an Ohio coal magnate named Mark Hanna retired from business to go into politics full time as William McKinley's mentor and manager.

Money proved helpful to any machine. Those rich enough to buy positions or nominations could do much of their own financing, and they frequently attracted contributions from other wealthy businessmen who trusted one of their own. Sometimes a railroad or industry would underwrite a candidate or even a whole state machine. The dynamic president of the Pennsylvania Railroad, Thomas A. Scott, played a major role in ensuring that legislators friendly to his railroad won re-election to the legislature at Harrisburg. Assessments on officeholders' salaries provided income for the machines as well. In addition, the machines developed many ethically questionable techniques for raising money. For example, a party leader might have a strike bill introduced in the state legislature. The bill would be designed to affect adversely a particular interest, so its operators would be forced to pay to have the bill killed. This process amounted to little more than blackmail on the part of the boss. Some money-making schemes involved the federal government and interstate operations. For example, the infamous Whiskey Ring, exposed when President Grant appointed an honest secretary of the treasury, Benjamin H. Bristow, diverted excise-tax revenue from the federal treasury into Republican party coffers.

Some of the money collected by the bosses inevitably went to line the pockets of avaricious partisans, but much was used to buy votes for the party. A class of men known as floaters carefully remained politically undecided until a partisan paid the right price for their votes. Floaters differed from independents, who voted as their consciences rather than their pocketbooks dictated. The state of Indiana reportedly contained an especially large and frequently purchased contingent of floaters. Both parties regularly set aside large sums of money to buy Hoosier votes. At a testimonial dinner following the election of 1880, Chester Arthur rashly toasted party manager Stephen W. Dorsey for his effective use of bribery in Indiana.

Another common characteristic of party politics, and the one upon which reformers focused their attention, was the machines' use of patronage to reward loyal service. Party workers expected to be compensated for their endeavors either with money or by being put forward for elective or appointive offices. Local government officials and state administrators appointed men to fill a number of jobs and also got to dictate the choice of appointees to some federal jobs in return for their support of the national party. Federal patronage was significant but not essential to the maintenance of state and local machines. The Democrats, who built increasingly powerful political organizations through the 1870's, had no control over the Republican Presidents nor any expectation that the Republicans would help them.

Control of a state was the most a machine could handle on a self-sustaining basis, and a United States senator usually operated such a machine or served its interests. In fact, the Senate resembled a sort of federation of state bosses. Michigan's Zachariah Chandler, the Pennsylvania Camerons, New York's Roscoe Conkling, Illinois's General John A. Logan, and Indiana's Oliver P. Morton were all Republican senators who simultaneously headed the dominant machine in their home states. The boss could often choose his Senate colleague from within the machine, as did Conkling in selecting his underling, Thomas C. Platt, to be the junior senator from New York. Each of these Senate bosses devoted a good portion of his time and energy to state politics. Until ratification of the Seventeenth Amendment in 1913, providing for popular election of senators, a man wishing to gain a Senate seat had to win the support of a majority of the state legislators. Consequently, no senator who hoped to retain his position could ignore local politics. Historian David J. Rothman, a student of Senate politics in the Gilded Age, has described the activities of Michigan Senator James McMillan in the 1880's and

1890's. An independently wealthy man, McMillan was able to send contributions ranging from $25 to $750 to a majority of the 132 candidates for the state legislature. He also financed and arranged such vote-getting techniques as providing free transportation to the polls. When the Republican legislative candidates won, they rewarded their benefactor by appointing him to the United States Senate. McMillan remained in constant touch with home politics while serving in the Senate.

Therefore, even members of the national Congress were never completely free of political responsibilities at home. Once an individual had constructed an apparatus to get himself into office, he carefully maintained and strengthened it for future needs. Furthermore, many vital political decisions were made at the state or local level. State legislatures continued to exercise the chartering authority, enabling political leaders to control business and industrial ventures. City and county administrators enjoyed a similar sort of power through local licensing regulations. As long as the state political organizations remained influential in determining the composition of the federal Congress, even national-interest groups and lobbyists had to devote some attention to local conditions. With the exception of tariff and money questions, the federal government exercised little responsibility in the area of business regulation.

Various state governments also developed new methods that would later spread to the federal government. During the 1870's and 1880's, agrarian-dominated legislatures in several Midwestern states experimented with state regulation of private enterprise. The Granger Laws of this period created a new role for government in which laws or regulatory agencies served the public interest by curbing unfair practices. The federal government eventually matched these state developments when it adopted the Interstate Commerce Commission Act in 1887 and the Sherman Antitrust Act in 1890. In the West, state governments instituted women suffrage and the direct election of senators long before such policies became nationwide. With a few noteworthy exceptions, such as the creation of a merit civil-service system, the federal government tended to follow rather than lead the states in political innovation.

For a brief period, during the Civil War, the central government had exercised enormous power. Congress, in the last two years of the war, appropriated more money than the legislature had in the whole span of the nation's history from 1789 to 1860. Heavy spending continued during military reconstruction, but, little by little, as the federal government dropped war-related or emergency programs, such as the Freedmen's Bureau, its energy and authority waned. By and large this gradually lowering federal profile suited the people. As the state and local governments continued their normal expansion of authority, the federal edifice found a new equilibrium, much lower than the one it had achieved during the frenetic war years. And, quite naturally, party activities followed suit, with state machines and local organizations remaining busy while the national party establishments did relatively less than before.

The comparative scope of the various levels of government is reflected in the size of their budgets. In 1880, state and local governments collected over $300 million in taxes of one kind or another to finance their operations. Because of its inflated tariff rates, the federal treasury collected about $360 million but spent only $260 million, half of that to pay veterans' benefits and interest on Civil War loans. Total federal outlays amounted to about five dollars per capita, while all other governments combined spent six dollars per person. As state and local government spending more than matched that of the federal government, the significance of local politics should not be underestimated. (The current situation is very different indeed. The national government is now spending approximately $1000 per person per year—about twice as much as all other forms of government combined. Even allowing for the vastly different value of money in the 1880's, it is apparent that government did not exert the pervasive influence on everyday life it does today.) Besides, there were plenty of opportunities for corruption and power at the local level. New York City alone employed some 10,000 persons in various capacities, and the city's budget in 1880 amounted to about half of the $56 million all nonfederal government agencies expended in New York State.

The patchwork of districts and divisions with overlapping or conflicting jurisdictions prevented the central government from dictating local policies. Each unit had its elected and appointed officials who jealously guarded their particular bailiwicks. The extreme states-rights doctrine had suffered a blow during the Civil War, but, after the deterioration of Radical Republican Reconstruction in the South, the federal government lost interest in imposing its will on local authorities. The party structures reflected the diversity of political units, and the national parties remained largely diversified into regional machines.

The federal government was, of course, larger than any single state's governing body, but it was far smaller than all elements of local government combined. Then as now, American voters elected only two men on a national basis, the President and the Vice-President. The winners of that election would exercise a good deal of power, but, because the government was much less active than it is today and operated with a correspondingly smaller bureaucracy, the President played a less crucial role in the over-all government structure. Furthermore, because the President traditionally divided his personal patronage among deserving members of his party, Senate and House leaders diluted his personal influence within the federal bureaucracy. This meant that the President, too, had to be responsive to local and state political problems to a large extent. The national party as such consisted of a confederation of principalities, and its organizational structure reflected this fact.

The national party did not maintain a constant existence in the manner of local machines. Each national convention created a national committee, usually including a leader from each state, and this committee provided the national party with its continuity. In practice, the party adhered through traditional loyalties and the constant operations of its local representatives, rather than through the activities of its national committee. In a process still followed today, the committee called itself together sometime prior to a national election for the purpose of selecting a location, a date, and some temporary officers for the party's Presidential nominating convention. The convention, meeting every four years, drew together representatives from the welter of state parties. The convention delegates approved a national platform, chose a Presidential nominee and a running mate, established a new national committee, and dissolved. From then on, the national committee chairman and his staff coordinated the functions of the national party. Most of the actual politicking and fund-raising took place through the efforts of local units of the party.

The leadership of both national parties during the last third of the nineteenth century consisted of alliances of bosses and local leaders. The parties lacked the central focus that had character-ized Jefferson's Republicans and Jackson's Democrats. The most influential party leaders were those who devoted their attention to state politics rather than the Presidency. The series of lack-luster Presidential contenders the Republicans nominated after 1872 did not represent an over-all weakness in the party so much as the strength of individual regional bosses. Whether the party's Presidential campaign ended in victory or defeat, it did not radi-cally alter the soundly functioning Republican machines through-out the nation.

A partisan's attitudes on certain issues did more to define his political position than did his party designation. How, then, did the parties manage to retain their members? No single leader attracted followers on a national basis, and, as Chapter 2 will show, after a time no single issue aligned the parties either. The persistence of the parties, then, depended upon widespread and overpowering loyalty to an abstraction. Ironically, this loyalty appeared to be growing stronger at a time when the parties were becoming more and more similar in their stands. Many of the short-lived third parties formed to support a particular principle announced their position in their names—e.g., the Greenback, Free Silver, and Prohibition parties. None of these could abandon the basic principle for which it had been named, but the deliber-ately obscure Democratic and Republican titles could stand for anything or nothing.

The Bloody Shirt has yet to be completely retired from service on either side of the Mason-Dixon Line, and in the immediate postwar years its ability to stir emotions was undeniable. Only the rise of a provocative new set of issues in the 1890's seriously challenged traditional party loyalties.

In any election, party loyalty did most of the machine's work for it. Thaddeus Stevens was reputed to have said, "throw con-science to the Devil and stand by your party," and even persons hostile to machines continued to vote the party line. Guaranteed the support of loyal voters, a party could survive no matter how

poorly it might do in a particular election. Independent or floating votes represented only a small portion of those regularly cast.
The unthinking, illiterate, or indifferent voter depended upon the
party label to help him decide how to vote. Contributions regularly flowed into campaign chests from men who lacked interest
in any particular benefit the party might provide them. Professional partisans benefited from party contributions, whatever
their source.

Not every loyal partisan ignored the flaws within his own
party. Many intelligent and honest men continued to support a
particular party in the fear that the opposing party would be
infinitely worse. No matter how much a member of one Republican faction might dislike the other factions, he could always
justify voting for one of them on the ground that, by definition,
any Democrat must be worse. Many nonprofessionals in politics
identified their party's interests precisely with those of the country. The vast majority of voters has behaved in much the same
way for the past hundred years. Perhaps the major change that
has occurred recently is that the percentage of declared independents has increased. Most of those who call themselves Democrats or Republicans today probably vote with just as much blind
faith as did their predecessors.

Undeviating loyalty to one of the nineteenth-century parties
tended to befog issues at all levels. On a ballot containing a long
list of local offices, the uninformed voter would quite often mark
as his choice unknown men simply on the basis of their party
designations. A partisan so elected might have no motivation
other than personal enrichment, but the party label sufficed to
boost him into office. Professional politicians could find many
ways of exploiting party loyalty for their own purposes. It has
been said that some party leaders, notably President Garfield and
his associates in the Republican party, encouraged party loyalty
in an attempt to rid the organization of dependence upon a
particular leader, such as Grant. The parties generally depended
for their strength simply upon their reputations and associations.

The strength of a national party's coalition of regional machines and organizations lay in its great diversity. A Southern
sharecropper had virtually nothing in common with a Northern

banker. Westerners differed from Easterners, the rich from the poor, farmers from industrialists. Each element of the party could adopt a national label and still concentrate its attention on local organizations for influence in state and national conventions. The party labels were so ambiguous that a particular machine could adopt a national label and still concentrate its attention on local problems. In the 1870's, Thomas A. Hendricks' Democratic party in Indiana advocated greenbacks and an increase in the nation's money supply. At the same time, Democrats in New York, led by Governor Samuel J. Tilden, favored a stable, gold-standard monetary system. At its 1876 Presidential nominating convention, the party chose a compromise slate with Tilden and Hendricks as running mates. The balanced ticket would presumably placate all who called themselves Democrats, regardless of their attitudes on the money question. Such ticket-balancing has remained common. One need only recall the 1960 Democratic ticket, which combined a liberal Easterner, John F. Kennedy, with a much more conservative Southwesterner, Lyndon Johnson.

The Gilded Age Republican party also encompassed competing and even contradictory interests. Not surprisingly, individuals who controlled their home districts played leading roles at national conventions. General John A. Logan created an impregnable political edifice in Illinois, founded upon his popularity with Union army veterans and his prominence in their organization, the Grand Army of the Republic. As long as he kept Union sentiments alive, Logan remained unbeatable in his state. Even when the national Republican party suffered the loss of the Presidency, as it did in 1884, Logan's army of supporters never defected. Such strong local organizations long thwarted the efforts of those who wished to destroy machine control of the national parties and create sound, compassionate, and idealistic government.

In fact, this was only one of a number of obstacles the opponents of machines faced. For some time, a number of competing political questions and proposals distracted the nation's attention. Until the politicians and the electorate resolved or lost interest in these other issues, reformers would encounter difficulties in getting a hearing for their proposals.

2. The Parties Achieve Parity

In America, the great moving forces are the parties. The government counts for less than in Europe, the parties count for more; and the fewer have become their principles and the fainter their interest in those principles, the more perfect has become their organization.

—JAMES BRYCE
The American Commonwealth (1888)

The growing influence party organizations exerted on government operations triggered criticism almost as soon as General Ulysses Grant took office as chief executive after the election of 1868. The popular war hero became President in little more than name, for he permitted party leaders to manage federal affairs from positions inside and outside his cabinet. This symbiotic arrangement broke down now and then, most notably when Radical Republican Senator Charles Sumner rejected Grant's plan to seize Santo Domingo. Generally, the Republicans managed to avoid any major political setbacks as they worked to perfect their party mechanisms during this period. Grant seldom bothered to try to understand what his self-appointed advisers were up to; he was content to reside placidly in the White House.

Outside the executive mansion, life was not so pleasant. The country was undergoing an exciting but rather reckless inflationary boom, which would collapse with disastrous consequences in 1873, shortly after President Grant's second term began. The war-engendered expansion of the federal government had created new agencies and civil servants capable of abusing and perverting government authority. The host of political leeches who fastened themselves to Grant's administration posed a danger to the national government and those it served, but the people were too preoccupied with reaping the profits of the postwar inflation or glorying in peace to care.

As Grant's first term drew toward its unavoidable electoral referendum in 1872, diverse elements, many within the Republican party itself, began to organize a protest movement. Some of the Republicans who led the anti-Grant crusade felt that the President had failed to give them a proper share of the patronage; others, led by Senator Carl Schurz of Missouri, simply considered the patronage system reprehensible. Thoroughly dedicated to reform, Schurz was also a professional politician. Born in Germany, he had left his homeland after participating in the unsuccessful revolution of 1848 and had become a strong advocate of the American system of democratic government. Since he was known to possess high personal ambitions within the political structure, he startled many of the more cautious reformers when he called for an outright repudiation of Grant. Schurz's enthusiasm proved vital to the formation of the Liberal Republican movement, dedicated to good government and the removal of Grant as head of the Republican party. Also, of course, Liberal Republican politicians, including Schurz, whom Grant's associates and advisers had kept out of control, hoped to gain positions of authority in an administrative reshuffle.

Those who were profiting under Grant's figurehead were equally insistent on blocking any change. The flamboyant New York boss, Senator Roscoe Conkling, headed Grant's beneficiaries, a group known as Stalwarts, whose entrenched power ensured that the party's convention would renominate the war hero. As Grant's renomination appeared to be inevitable, disgruntled partisans called a separate meeting under the Liberal Republican banner. Those who attended this ad hoc convention shared only one clear motivation: a desire to oust Grant. The Liberal Republican sponsors exercised no control over who participated; the assemblage thus consisted of a jumble of individuals whom the regular parties had ignored. Idealistic charter members of the prewar Republican party mingled with proponents of a wide variety of special interests, among them advocates of free trade, less militant reconstruction of the South, civil-service reform, and scores of other proposals. According to historian Matthew Josephson, the convention was "almost equally composed of amateurs and political crooks."

This motley crowd adopted a platform protesting a multitude of evils, many of them associated with the Grant Administration. The Liberal Republicans appeared to be less interested in fostering an alternative party than in criticizing the whole existing party system. Through a process that appalled the more idealistic participants, the convention nominated Horace Greeley for the Presidency. Greeley had long since lost the respect of the more conscientious reformers for, during his many years as editor of the *New York Tribune*, he had espoused almost every reform scheme ever proposed, no matter how fanciful. He had been a Unionist and he disliked Grant, but that about exhausted his list of qualifications. He advocated much higher protective tariffs, a stand that contradicted the Liberal Republican platform just adopted. Emotionally committed reformers like Schurz swallowed their disappointment and stayed with the mortally wounded Liberal Republican coalition. Other Republicans did not hate Grant enough to favor the Liberal alternative and so slipped back quietly into the regular party. Those reformers who perceptively noted that it was not Grant but his advisers who had caused the corruption never dropped out of the regular party at all.

As if to limit further Greeley's appeal to the Republicans, the Democratic party shortly afterward also nominated the irascible editor, hoping to capitalize on his well-known opposition to Grant. In the end, the Liberal Republican protest had done little but upstage the Democrats and help the disgruntled to work off steam. Despite frenetic efforts on Greeley's part, Grant's supporters swept the General into office again. Although his opponents had largely brought on their own defeat, the President appeared to be convinced that he had proved his popularity in a meaningful race. Consequently, Grant felt that he need make few changes in his administrative policies. The Liberal Republicans were worse off than before, since loyal partisans now treated them as pariahs.

The reformers' ignominious defeat provoked a great deal of analysis and criticism. Obviously, a better candidate would have helped tremendously. Beyond that, the campaign proved how powerful the machines had become. The more perspicacious reformers realized that they would have to coordinate their efforts more effectively if any future attempt to overthrow the spoilsmen was to succeed. Unfortunately, the diversity of views in evidence at the Liberal Republican Convention made the selection of a single positive issue impossible. In 1872, too many other considerations competed with the pursuit of political reform. Free traders and protectionists, Radical Reconstructionists and Redeemers, soft- and hard-money advocates, all seemed too devoted to their own programs to cooperate with one another. The resulting chaotic coalition had produced a political disaster. The strength and survival of a party depends in part upon its ability to compromise its internal differences. The Liberal Republican Convention had failed to accomplish this essential unification.

The gradual disappearance of partisan issues during the 1870's significantly helped those who wished to fight the selfish political organizations. As fewer vital issues separated the parties, their excesses appeared in a clearer light. A Unionist might feel a responsibility to vote for a somewhat corrupt Republican party engaged in saving the Union from dissolution, but such a responsibility lapsed when the Democratic platform and candidates differed very little from those of the Republican party. Habit or expectation of reward motivated a degree of loyalty among the bulk of the partisans, but neither influenced the man who wished to follow his own conscience. What eventually developed on the political scene closely resembled that seldom-achieved hypothetical situation in which all other things *were* equal. One could vote for whichever nominee he liked or whichever party edged closer to his views on the particular issue that interested him most.

Constant political debate and frequent election campaigns would never permit all issues to die out completely. Although the federal government accomplished very little except routine administration in the period from 1872 to 1893, politicians continually attempted to drum up partisan interest and enthusiasm. The crisis mentality that had so recently characterized political life faded away very slowly. After the Radical Reconstruction process had begun to collapse under the distracted Grant regime, controversies over tariffs or money policies developed, and some politicians attempted to base their political careers on a particular stand, such as advocacy of higher tariffs. But such actions were futile. The slackening interest in other issues permitted reformers to build up steam behind their own pet issue and helped them to get a hearing for their views.

The problem that had dominated all aspects of American life for years was, of course, sectionalism. The North-South conflict persisted through the immediate postwar years, while the Radicals attempted to ensure political and economic equality to the blacks the Republican party had freed from slavery. This effort necessarily interfered with a quieting of tensions, for it meant the continued involvement of Northerners in Southern affairs. The federal troops who occupied the South protected Radical Republican governments in that area. White Southerners, of course, bitterly objected to those they considered outsiders and traitors controlling their governments. Southerners who advocated the termination of Radical control throughout the former Confederacy became known as Redeemers. Several sorts of protest groups sprang up at this time, including the Ku Klux Klan. Some of these groups intimidated the newly enfranchised blacks into voting their way or not going to the polls at all. Once federal troops withdrew from various Southern states, Republican control exited as well. By 1872, the Redemption period had begun as Democratic Redeemers replaced Republican-sponsored governments. By 1877, Redemption was complete.

The Democrats' success in restructuring and recapturing political control in the South resulted in part from a loss of interest in the North. Maintaining the South as a satrapy of Northern interests involved a lot of hard work. The blacks required instruction and protection. Many prewar abolitionists gave up hope of the speedy assimilation of blacks into white society after frustrating dealings with the freedmen. While Northerners found controlling the South an increasingly onerous task, Southerners eagerly awaited a chance to take up the burden. The postwar economic boom distracted attention from the well-worn sectional issue, and the subsequent financial panic in 1873 diverted men's minds still more. Those who tried to revive the old sectional emotionalism seemed increasingly insincere. The issue inevitably reappeared during political campaigns but with gradually decreasing effectiveness.

So long as Grant remained President, however, the Civil War issues could not be laid to rest. On various pretexts, federal troops continued to occupy some parts of the South; the once-predominant Republican control decayed under the Redeemers' onslaughts, but it did not totally disappear. The Southern Democratic party was clearly on the upswing, and it would soon occupy a pre-eminent position throughout the section. Once they could complete the Redemption process, the Democrats would be able to settle back into virtually uncontested control. The solid Democratic South would become a permanent feature of the nation's political picture.

Meanwhile, the Northern Democratic party was shaking off its wartime image as the refuge of faint-hearted Unionists or outright friends of the rebelling South. Democrats were busily re-establishing enclaves in the loyal states. Once New Jersey Democrats took control of the governorship in 1869, they retained it without interruption for twenty-seven years. Connecticut voters elected Democratic administrations intermittently from 1867 on. By the early 1870's, both Ohio and Indiana had followed suit. Ohio Democrats had helped to elect a series of Union party governors up to 1868; in the 1870's they supported straight Democratic tickets. New York's wartime governor, Democrat Horatio Seymour, had given Grant a good run for the Presidency in 1868, and a Tammany-sponsored Democrat, John T. Hoffman, won the gubernatorial race in the Empire State that same year. Hoffman was re-elected in 1870, and the Republicans finally had to coerce an elderly Democrat named John A. Dix to run on their ticket in order to defeat their Democratic opponents. The victory was short-lived, however, for the Democrats ran a Reform Democrat named Samuel J. Tilden for governor in 1874 and easily displaced the Republican administration.

Tilden had become nationally famous for his successful fight against the most corrupt political boss in the United States, Democrat William Marcy Tweed. Tweed had managed to take control of the New York City-based Tammany Hall organization in the late 1860's. From 1868 until his arrest in late 1871, Tweed ran the city as a dictator. In addition, while his agent, John T. Hoffman, was governor of New York, Tweed had a seat in the state senate, making certain that no legislation detrimental to his operations in the city was approved. His ring was reputed to have stolen between $40 million and $200 million from the city. Tweed's operation obtained some of its illegal funds by siphoning off the city's tax receipts and much of the rest in the form of kickbacks from city contractors and employees.

Samuel Tilden, a very able lawyer who was serving as Democratic state committee chairman in 1871, had been alienated by Tweed's tactics and was determined to oust the political boss from power. Backed by businessmen and others either envious of Tweed's success or nauseated by his methods, Tilden eventually succeeded in exposing Tweed's corruption and sending him to prison. The crusading Tilden received much help from the reform press in the city, including the *New York Times* and *Harper's Weekly*. Although Tilden himself was an accomplished professional politician, his victory over Tweed gave him the reputation of a reformer. This and the influence of Democratic associates throughout the state won him the governorship. In office, Tilden increased his popularity by his impartial administration of the nation's most populous state. The Democratic party, which had been so short on leaders in 1872 that it had merely endorsed the Liberal Republican's nominee, now bounced back with Tilden as its Presidential choice.

The opposition panicked. The Redeemers had severely weakened the Republican hold on the South, while the Democratic party was reviving throughout the North. The depression that began in 1873 had helped the Democrats to win their first post-war majority in the House of Representatives a year later. Republican leaders acknowledged dismal prospects for the upcoming Presidential sweepstakes. On one hand, the Stalwarts, those who had prospered so much from their manipulation of the Grant Administration, favored a third term for the general. On the other hand, a group of partisans known as Half-Breeds, perhaps no less unprincipled than Grant's henchmen, wanted a share in the control of the national party. As long as Grant remained in office, the chance of any change that would benefit them seemed slight. They hoped that by electing a new President they could move in and reap the advantages in patronage, influence, and programs that Grant's supporters had enjoyed. Consequently, they proposed a Radical Senator from Maine, James G. Blaine, instead. As a former Speaker of the House, Blaine possessed a substantial national following.

At the 1876 Republican national convention, the usual array of favorite sons and self-seeking bosses did nothing but deepen the factional split. The Grant and Blaine forces finally compromised on the nomination of the respectable, but not widely known, governor of Ohio, Rutherford B. Hayes. The Liberal Republican remnant, most of whom had been reassimilated into the party, was favorably disposed toward Hayes. As he had been a Union general, his advocates made much of this throughout the campaign. The Republican party continued to capitalize on the sectional disturbances that had promoted it to power in the first place and had paid such ample rewards during Reconstruction.

The Democratic nominee, Tilden, preferred to leave the campaigning to his supporters and his running mate, Thomas A. Hendricks, a former Copperhead from Indiana. Hendricks' sympathetic attitude toward the South attracted those who wanted the Democratic party to rise again. The Democrats tried to capitalize on Republican corruption, while the Republicans hammered away at the Democratic war record. In fact, Hayes and Tilden stood quite close to each other on basic political principles, their differences being more of degree than of kind. The hoopla surrounding the campaign did not conceal the fact that the two American political parties had fallen into balance, a condition that would persist until 1896. The election's inconclusive aftermath did, however, raise serious questions about the viability of the nation's political system and the stability of the Union itself.

A brief review of the familiar story of the disputed election of 1876 indicates its importance as a watershed. The electoral count was so close that a few votes could give the victory to either party. An election-night tally showed 184 uncontested votes for Tilden and 165 for Hayes. Both the Democrats and the Republicans claimed to have won in three Southern states, Louisiana, South Carolina, and Florida, which together possessed nineteen votes. These, coupled with an additional disputed electoral vote from Oregon, would have been sufficient to provide Hayes with a one-vote plurality. The three contested Southern states still suffered the vestiges of Radical Reconstruction in the form of federal occupation troops. Protected by these military forces, Republican canvassing boards turned in results favorable to Hayes, while Democratic spokesmen insisted that their candidate had won. In Washington, the Democratic House of Representatives debated the Republican-controlled Senate over whose reports should be accepted. The two houses finally agreed to create an electoral commission to determine the winner. The members voted along party lines to give Hayes the semblance of a legitimate victory. The sectional split appeared to be alive and well.

Amid rumors of the imminent renewal of the Civil War, thoughtful Democratic leaders took stock of the situation. Many of them, particularly in the South, had been prewar Whigs who favored the same economic programs the Republicans had developed for the North. The Democrats concluded that they could gain valuable concessions in return for agreeing to let Hayes move into the White House, so they struck a compromise that gave the Republicans the Presidency. In return they obtained assurance of the withdrawal of all remaining troops from the South as well as promises of support for Southern economic-development proposals. The occupation would doubtless have ended shortly in any case, but everyone appeared to have gained something in the deal. The Republicans got the White House, Southern Democrats completed the Redemption, and the nation was relieved of some abrasive remnants of the sectional crisis. The peaceful compromise of 1877 brought to a close the period of emotional sectionalism that had triggered the Civil War. Sectional feeling persisted, but it no longer dominated national thinking. The solid Democratic South became an accepted fact of political life, and the politicians sought other issues with which to stir the electorate.

The frenzy of government activity that accompanied the war had produced many substantial changes in American political attitudes. Among the most controversial was the acceptance of the high protective tariff. The Republicans had actually passed the first high tariff bill even before the fighting broke out to reward industrial supporters who wanted protection from foreign competition. As wartime exigencies demanded ever-increasing amounts of money, Congress found raising the tariffs an acceptable method of producing needed revenue. Frequently boosted upward during the war, rates remained high afterwards. The Republican protection policies pleased many industrialists in the Northeast, who swung labor into line with the argument that wage rates would drop if American manufactures had to compete with untaxed foreign goods. The Democratic party had historically opposed high tariffs, and it generally continued to favor lower rates. A few free-traders were sprinkled in both major parties. Having raised the rates initially, however, the Republican party continued to advocate high duties.

The tariffs had several economic consequences. Industrialists made fortunes by charging high prices. American laborers may or may not have received higher wages as a consequence. Consumers had to pay the high prices protective rates induced, but no one paid much attention to consumer attitudes at that time. The most ridiculous consequence of the high rates was that the federal government continued to collect vast amounts of money it did not need through its customs operations. A necessity during wartime, the excess revenue embarrassed politicians, who could not devise pork-barrel schemes fast enough to dispose of it. Blaine, for one, cleverly suggested ways of using up the surplus, reviving the old Jacksonian proposal of doling out federal money to the state governments, a plan which would in turn reduce local taxation. This same proposal, now called revenue sharing, has recently been suggested once again to help states meet their budgetary needs. (The current proposals do not stem from federal surpluses, however, but rather from the federal government's efficiency in tax collecting in comparison to that of the state governments.) The depression of the 1870's helped to reduce the treasury surplus, but it remained an undesirable outgrowth of the politically profitable high tariff rates. No significant changes in the rates occurred until the Republicans further increased the tariffs in 1890, although a Republican-controlled Congress engineered a meaningless reform tariff in a lame-duck session in 1883. Tariffs never stimulated as much excitement as the Bloody Shirt had, and they hardly rated as an issue of crucial national interest.

Another war-magnified issue that came closer to home for many Americans concerned the money supply. The average citizen had ample reason to worry, for the per-capita money supply did not increase at nearly the same pace as other economic indicators. A limited supply of currency meant lower wages and decreasing farm prices. After President Andrew Jackson killed the Second Bank of the United States in the 1830's, the federal government had generally stayed out of the money market. The Civil War emergencies required something a good deal more reliable than the subtreasury system and state banks could offer. As an expedient, both Confederate and Union governments issued paper money by fiat. The Northern bills became known as greenbacks to distinguish them from the orange-printed gold certificates also in circulation. Congress had authorized the printing of $450 million worth of greenbacks by the end of the war, but the amount in circulation never rose that high. Subsequent legislation stabilized it at just under $350 million. Paper money proved popular with debtors because it generally cost less than gold and they could therefore obtain it more easily for the liquidation of debts. In the 1870's a rural-labor political coalition called the Greenback party was formed specifically to encourage the government to issue more of this cheap paper money. Instead, in a series of brilliant financial strokes, Republican administrators stabilized the amount in circulation and then announced that, as of January, 1879, the treasury would exchange gold for greenbacks at par. With the greenbacks limited in quantity and thus made as good as gold, they were no longer the palliative cheap-money advocates in the Greenback party desired. After 1880, greenbacks ceased to be a major political issue.

As the greenback controversy faded away, free silver assumed some prominence. This monetary expedient became feasible in the late 1870's, when the nation's silver production increased to such an extent that the metal's price dropped below the treasury's legally set standard of sixteen ounces of silver to one of gold. Demands arose from the mining regions for free and unlimited coinage of silver, and the cheap-money advocates took up the cry. Such a program would add significantly to the nation's money supply. Conservative Republican Senator William B. Allison of Iowa outflanked the silverites by setting a limit on the amount of coinage that the bill proposed by Missouri Representative Richard P. Bland would have permitted. The 1878 Bland-Allison Silver Purchase Act settled the issue for twelve years. Only in the 1890's would free silver again emerge as a leading political issue.

Both tariffs and the money supply represented aspects of the more fundamental problem of the country's economic ill health. The inflationary boom that preceded the panic of 1873 merely intensified the impact of the subsequent depression. Americans were shocked and confused by the destruction and death associated with the national railroad strike of 1877. The farmers had to wait impatiently until the early twentieth century to enjoy what they considered an acceptable level of prosperity. Yet the government appeared to be uninterested in doing anything about this depression or the series of less severe recessions that punctuated the 1880's. Only in the trough of the downturn in the 1890's did the federal government take strong measures, and those measures unfortunately merely intensified the problem. Economic suffering persisted while politicians debated whether they should shift irrelevant tariff rates up or down. As the government did nothing, the political parties seldom concerned themselves with the nation's economic woes either.

In fact, the political parties at the national level seemed most concerned with how best to get their members re-elected. At the state and local levels, politicians carried on business as usual. The emphasis lay not on what the government should do but on how it should be done. Freed from more pressing worries, the parties attempted to manufacture interest in their empty platforms, substituting showmanship for substance, while leading partisans devoted their energies to shaping their machines. Factions sprang up, but differences among them often revolved around the question of which set of bosses should control the spoils. In retrospect, the supporters of Grant appear to have been the most unprincipled, but perhaps only because they had eight untrammeled years to explore fully the opportunities for corruption. Envy of that capability for corruption in part motivated some of those who opposed a third term for the General, as they occupied the unsatisfying position of being outs when their own party was in.

The close balance between the Democrats and Republicans encouraged third parties and determined interest groups to aspire to control the swing votes. Greenbackers in the House of Representatives accomplished just that in the late 1870's, and others would try to do the same in the future. At best, this balance between the parties may have limited the ambitions of the more blatant spoilsmen: the close margin of victory could have frightened the winner into some semblance of responsibility.

This concentration on how the governmental system operated rather than on what it should do had long-run consequences for the party system. While bosses tinkered with their machines, others debated alternative methods of influencing public opinion. In the absence of insistent national issues, reformers, idealists, and other outs all tried to reverse the trend toward self-seeking control of the parties. Yet that same absence of issues permitted the politicians to devote their energies in the opposite direction. Reform of the civil service assumed a leading position in the critics' planning. The corruption of party organizations seemed linked to one major flaw in the system: the abuse of the patronage power. The crisis atmosphere that had permitted and encouraged such abuse had dissipated. Profiteering or slipshod management might inevitably accompany wartime emergencies, but those emergencies no longer existed. Many men, both inside and outside politics, felt that the time had come to do away with the overblown apparatus the war crisis had produced. Reform of the civil service appeared to be the best means of accomplishing that goal.

3. The Rise of Reform

We had laid our hands on the barbaric palace of patronage and begun to write on its walls, Mene, mene! *Nor, I believe, will the work end till they are laid in the dust.*

—GEORGE WILLIAM CURTIS, addressing the founding session of the National Civil Service Reform League, August, 1881

The machine system and its corrupt tendencies bothered a good many people, including some in the decision-making centers of the parties. Yet the usefulness and effectiveness of machine organization made reform from inside the parties unlikely. Realizing that what they considered a cancer would never heal itself, idealists floundered around for a weapon or a program that would reduce the power of the machines. Both the British and the Prussian governments were involved in establishing merit systems for their bureaucrats, and the Imperial Chinese Customs Service provided an excellent example of a professional civil service. Many of the reform advocates in the United States were Anglophiles more than willing to copy the successes of Victorian reforms. Those who had served in the army during the war had personally experienced a system in which, at least to some degree, merit meant promotion and incompetence drew retribution. Unfortunately, advocates of change encountered great obstacles in attempting to popularize a foreign or military ideal among democratic, nativist Americans. The United States was very hesitant to bestir itself in the direction of reform.

Some of the advocates of civil-service reform expected their program to create an efficient, nonpartisan bureaucracy. This group hoped that a merit system would keep incompetents out of government service and attract honest, qualified men. Other reformers expected it to eliminate the evils inherent in a spoils system based on partisanship. They felt that removing the distribution of government offices from the control of party bosses would destroy the bosses' chief means of support and power. As the reformers never made it clear whether their main goal was the establishment of a better administrative organization or the destruction of the machine system, they never seemed certain that they had accomplished their purpose. But, whatever they considered their ultimate goals, the reformers did agree that a reformed civil-service system represented a step in the right direction.

To a large degree, the two goals were complementary: a diminution in machine control would probably bring about a governmental system more acceptable to the reformers. Therefore, the most immediate concern had to do with revising the way in which the President staffed the executive branch. Partly as a result of the tremendous expansion of the federal government during the war, the President had to fill more than 100,000 federal offices. According to the Constitution, he could select his advisers and staff his cabinet departments in any manner he chose. Many Presidential appointees were subject to senatorial confirmation, but the majority eluded even that hurdle. An incoming President in the Gilded Age thus had to make an enormous number of decisions.

Quite obviously, no single man could decide rationally how to distribute so many jobs. In the traditional system that had developed, the President usually tackled the distribution problem on three levels. At the top were the cabinet members and the immediate advisers whom the President, in consultation with party leaders, chose himself. The President also dealt personally with a large number of lesser appointments. Many a President-elect used this direct approach to reward his personal staff and friends as well as his loyal campaign workers. The reformed civil-service system has never interfered much with the President's personal choices.

The second level of distribution included those appointments that the President felt called upon to make either to reward past political performance or to encourage future political assistance. Within each of the cabinet departments, one or more officials doled out jobs to benefit the chief executive. These officials usually held relatively obscure positions in their departments, but had tremendous power. Republicans in this period considered the South a vast rotten borough, which the President could exploit for personal gain. This attitude enabled President Rutherford Hayes to search out qualified former Whigs to appoint to federal offices in the hope that they would ultimately remain loyal to the Republican party. When Chester Arthur became President upon the death of Hayes' successor, James A. Garfield, he had little political support. One of his first moves was to appoint William E. Chandler of New Hampshire his secretary of the navy. Within a couple of years, Chandler and his associates in Washington had filled hundreds of federal offices throughout the South with men loyal to Arthur. This guaranteed the incumbent President a strong basis of support at the 1884 nominating convention.

The final level of distribution represented the real focus of the reform movement. Here were the jobs which the President distributed at his discretion to the various bosses and machines. Under informal agreements, representatives and senators as well as other state leaders were permitted to suggest federal appointees, usually for offices in the boss's home district. This system obviously worked to the President's advantage in obtaining congressional confirmation of his own choices for other positions. A tradition called senatorial courtesy had developed in which the President was expected to consult the senior senator from a particular state before announcing any appointments in that state. Some plums of the spoils system supposedly belonged to a particular boss—for example, the New York Customhouse, which

Grant had turned over to Roscoe Conkling. Fear of losing it would have motivated the boss to call for a third term for Grant even if he had no other interest in the matter.

Typically, a congressman received the right to select several hundred federal appointees and thus could easily reward his supporters and the members of his machine. Those jobs that the boss did not need as rewards for his friends were often sold to the highest bidder. In an ad in the *Washington Star* in 1885, for example, a wealthy officeseeker offered $500 for any position in the federal service not subject to civil-service restrictions; another offered three times that amount for the post of consul at Gothenburg, Sweden. The fortunate congressman with a few spare offices could simply sell them and pocket the proceeds. The lure of the salary and other emoluments that went with a consular or customs office made the jobs readily marketable.

Besides the obvious potential for corruption inherent in such a system, reformers considered it very inefficient. Not only did congressmen frequently select unqualified individuals for important federal posts, but the legislators had to devote a good deal of their own time to distribution problems. The National Civil Service Reform League, founded in 1881, reported a decade later its finding that each congressman personally made about 250 appointments. On the bulk of local offices, such as postmasters, tax collectors, and the like, the President simply rubber-stamped local representatives' decisions. To fill these posts, the average congressman dealt with over 1,000 applicants and spent more than a third of his time on patronage matters alone. The task of selecting among applicants became infinitely easier if one represented a machine that provided the names of deserving partisans. Ironically, the machine's screening of applicants actually freed congressmen from some of the drudgery of patronage work and enabled them to devote more attention to issues and proposals.

No President was entirely fair or equitable in distributing offices. Each one frankly and openly used the spoils as a means of keeping his partisans in line. One of the most important holds the executive had over congressmen and senators was his ability to grant or withhold patronage. Every now and then a President would permit or even encourage a member of his cabinet to intro-duce a merit system within his department, as, for example when Hayes let Carl Schurz, his Secretary of the Interior, establish a reformed system for appointments and tenure. More often than not, however, the President manipulated the spoils to his advan-tage.

It was a two-way street. If a machine had a sound basis in a given locale, it could often perpetuate its power even without Presidential assistance. Furthermore, bosses in the doubtful states could essentially blackmail the President, forcing him to lavish patronage on areas that were threatening to swing away from him or his party at the next election. Because of this incessant pressure from the doubtful states, almost all of them in the North or East, citizens from those states gained a disproportionate share of the offices in the federal bureaucracy. Consequently, congressmen from the West and South generally did not favor changes in the tenure provisions for federal officeholders. If those Easterners already in office were protected from removal by a civil-service program, they would be able to make permanent their control of government operations.

Regardless of how deplorable the spoils system was and how widespread the criticism directed against it, getting legislative action on it proved quite difficult. One could hardly expect con-gressmen to divest themselves of power. They dismissed the reform call as the work of outs angry at being denied a share of the spoils. This simplistic explanation might apply to some of the reform advocates, but it overlooked the sincere and idealistic motives of those who led the movement. Some considered the spoils system a great disaster that had befallen the American ex-periment in democracy. They hoped that a positive change would not only eliminate the disaster but would also improve the health and efficiency of the system. Some argued that no distribution of spoils, as such, should be made, feeling that federal offices should never be treated as booty for a band of plunderers. A reformer might possess any sort of motivation, however, and as many moti-vations existed as there were reformers.

The confluence of two major trends in American political de-velopment that occurred at this time had a great deal to do with the rousing of reform sentiment. The first trend, already discussed, was the maturation of self-seeking party machines. The second involved the growing complexity of government in a rapidly industrializing nation. In earlier days, political leaders assumed that almost anyone could handle a government job effectively. If indeed it had ever been valid, this assumption was obviously no longer warranted. The all-steel, steam-powered navy Congress approved in 1881 provides an excellent example. The new ships could never be built, repaired, or even adequately serviced in the antiquated navy yards. Modern naval technology required supervision by trained engineers, and the patronage-staffed navy yards had to change radically. Similar modernization in other areas led to a need for experts at all levels of government service.

Those who already feared that government administration suffered because of the corruption of spoilsmen now had an additional concern. The tasks officeholders had to perform were becoming increasingly complex, while bosses continued to nominate men of doubtful capabilities. An illiterate postal worker could hardly cope with his job, yet scarcely better-educated bosses often thrust illiterates forward for political reward. As time went on, even the bosses began to acknowledge that just anyone would not do for every job.

Unfortunately, the notion that any man can fill a government job has not completely died out. Most civil servants today are responsible and reasonably well qualified, but where appointive power remains unrestricted, the old concept prevails. Presidents still frequently choose cabinet officers for their political reliability and reputation rather than because they possess sound training and experience in government affairs. Furthermore, the President himself is often poorly trained for all the duties he has to perform, his major qualification being only that he had enough political savvy to get nominated and elected.

Reform of the civil service would not totally dissipate the President's appointive power; nor did the reformers want that. The President had to have some patronage to dole out in order to threaten punishment or promise reward for the members of his party. In addition, the various bosses down the line used the patronage positions for their own purposes. A boss might promise a man a job if he would work for the machine, and often this work continued even after the partisan had taken the job. One investigation revealed that some 200 employees collecting federal paychecks at the New York Customhouse did nothing but perform services for Conkling's machine. If they no longer had the hope of advancement either through elective or appointive office, many partisans might cease to concern themselves with essential party functions. Although subject to frequent abuse, therefore, the spoils did help to keep the party system running, and even the most outspoken critics of the abuses of the system were willing to have party government continue. They merely wanted to limit the selfishness of the party organizations so that better government and less partisanship would result.

The federal spoils system was not inherently dangerous. At its worst, Grant's administration did not destroy the nation. Compared to the present-day situation, the federal government in the 1870's and 1880's exercised little direct influence on the average citizen. The bosses did not threaten the lives or the welfare of most Americans, and anyone who really wished to avoid associating with machines probably could do so. On the other hand, the same individual might willingly risk dealing with a boss if he could perceive a personal or business advantage. Cooperation with a party organization usually involved a voluntary decision which could be reversed voluntarily as well. Whereas politics and campaigning aroused great enthusiasm among the electorate, government operations themselves had no particular popular appeal. Although most citizens might abstractly consider honest government desirable, only a minority of them considered reform of vital importance. The reformers took themselves quite seriously, of course, and felt that they would eventually save the nation from its debilitating political leadership. They urged the voters to interest themselves in reform and to encourage their legislators to act upon it.

The complexities of the party structure lay open several alternatives to determined reformers. The basic program had to do with the establishment of a merit system for the civil service in which hiring, promotion, and tenure would be based on a man's qualifications and demonstrated work capability, not on his party identification. The merit-system idea required legislation and appropriations, as well as a willingness on the part of administrators to make it work. Applicants would take competitive exams, and the individual earning the best score would be hired, regardless of his political affiliations. Such a system would presumably bring a better type of man forward, interest educated people in public service, and result in a more conscientious administration of government.

A simpler alternative, which might be integrated into a merit system, involved ending the periodic removal of civil servants for partisan reasons. Regardless of how a man had obtained his job, if he were functioning effectively in it, the reformers felt that he should not be thrown out simply because he had once worked for another party. A President who was willing to consider such a policy found that an old law tied his hands. Near the dawn of the party system, in 1820, Congress had passed the so-called Four Years Law, which limited tenure in certain federal offices to four years. Even if no party changeover occurred, many offices automatically became vacant. A competent officeholder might win another four-year appointment, but he had no guarantee. Once the basic merit system had been introduced, reformers devoted some attention to getting the Four Years Law repealed to provide job security for deserving officeholders not covered by the new system.

An aspect of the spoils system that legislative action alone seemed unable to prevent had to do with the contributions officeholders made to party campaign chests. The size of the kickback ranged from as little as 2 per cent of the salary to 10 per cent or even more, depending upon the emoluments associated with the office. A partisan who had been rewarded for his efforts with a job in the government recognized his duty to reciprocate by contributing to the party. Both national and local party leaders levied assessments, and these funds were more or less willingly paid. The money collected went into the machines' operating budgets, and was used to obtain the elective offices through which the patronage was funneled. Thus, in a sense, the parties milked the federal government for operating funds.

As indicated previously, an officeholder also would often

neglect his government work to do party tasks. The bosses did not necessarily consider this practice unethical. Political work ensured the health of the party, and if the party's interests were regarded as synonymous with those of the nation, the federal payroll was well spent. The reformers naturally rejected this reasoning and called for an end to obligatory contributions and party work. Presidential orders went out to this effect, but contributions continued to roll in, and partisan tasks continued to be performed. In the end, a professional civil service free from all partisan obligations seemed the best solution to all these abuses. Its advocates saw the merit system as the universal panacea for partisan mismanagement.

Stirrings of reform appeared in the late 1860's. Until he was defeated in an election in 1870, Rhode Island Representative Thomas A. Jenckes spent several years fruitlessly suggesting the establishment of a merit system. Influential Radical Senator Charles Sumner of Massachusetts espoused the reform cause, probably in part simply to embarrass the incumbent Presidents who depended heavily upon patronage manipulation to build support for themselves. Senator Lyman Trumbull of Illinois, a moderate Republican, also agitated in favor of denying congressmen control of Presidential appointments. Reconstruction hassles generally overshadowed these tentative first efforts. The dominant bosses were involved in the intricate process of strengthening their control of their machines inside the parties and would have nothing to do with schemes aimed at limiting it.

Of those involved in early attempts at political reform, President Grant seems one of the most unlikely. Although he frequently ignored their counsel, Grant had many advisers, including George William Curtis, an aristocratic literateur who favored a merit system. In its 1871 lame-duck session, the Forty-First Congress approved a rider to an appropriations bill authorizing the President to appoint a civil-service commission to establish rules for competitive examinations. Grant promptly appointed Curtis to head the advisory board. Beginning its operations in the summer of 1871, the commission maintained a tenuous existence for several years as part of the federal apparatus, devising the elements of a merit system for federal job applicants. President Grant tried some of the commission's suggestions, but as his administration wore on, the reform concept encountered increasing congressional criticism. By 1874, opponents had cut off all of the commission's operating funds, and what had begun as an optimistic experiment drowned in the corrupt tide of the General's Presidency.

Meanwhile the abortive Liberal Republican revolt had drawn attention to the evils of the spoils system. Once the Democrats took control of the House of Representatives in 1875, they tried to weaken the Republican stranglehold on the spoils by passing a law forbidding the confiscation of officeholders' salaries for party purposes. Implementation of this legislation, which Republican reformers praised, depended upon the President's attitude. The friends of the merit system hoped to make certain that a man sympathetic to their principles would become chief executive. As we have noted, the conflict between Grant's supporters and his opponents resulted in a reform nominee of sorts. Running on a platform that included a strong reform plank, Rutherford B. Hayes did little to further his own election. After Hayes' inauguration, the reformers waited expectantly for action. He eventually issued an executive order forbidding federal employees from actively participating in politics. Yet Senate investigators later discovered that, with Hayes' approval, a Republican congressional campaign committee had sent three letters to officeholders in 1878 asking for "voluntary contributions" to the party. A few may have risked their jobs and refused to pay, but any substantial change in the old practices clearly depended upon extensive reform.

Chosen as a compromise candidate, Hayes succeeded in alienating almost everyone in the Republican party. He put together a sound cabinet and permitted his Secretary of the Interior, reform advocate Carl Schurz, to adopt merit rules for the workers in his own department. But simultaneously, Secretary of the Treasury John Sherman judiciously tailored the patronage in his department to benefit himself. Thus the Hayes record on reform appeared mixed. If nothing else, Schurz's services in the cabinet restored his party respectability and inferentially tended to absolve all Liberal Republicans of the sins of 1872. By the end of the decade, ex-Liberal Republican reformers could once again move in the party's inner circles.

In one area, the President acted in a more assertive manner than the most optimistic reformers could have expected. The New York Customhouse produced the most profits of all the federal spoils. In the process of charging shipowners the appropriate tariffs on their imports, the customs officers also worked for their own benefit. The lucrative moiety system by which the collector stood to receive one-third of the profits from the sale of a condemned cargo had been abolished in 1874, but plenty of other money-making schemes existed. Clerks and assessors routinely received bribes from importers and shippers. In return, the customhouse employees either undervalued shipments, thus reducing the size of the tax levy, or let goods in without charging any duties at all. The collector and other high-ranking officials made a good deal of money out of what was called the general order business. According to the regulations, the agent or wholesaler importing goods had just one day after his goods had been unloaded to pay the duties and collect his wares. Under a general order the collector issued, customs agents transferred all unclaimed goods to government warehouses. To reclaim goods thus stored, the importer often had to pay arbitrarily set fees for storage and cartage. Despite periodic and exhaustive investigations, customs officials always seemed able to find loopholes or to exploit ambiguities in the tariff acts. So profitable was the operation that whoever controlled the New York Customhouse had the inside track in seeking to control political activities throughout the whole state. Senator Roscoe Conkling's minions, including Collector Chester A. Arthur and Naval Officer Alonzo B. Cornell, were administering this patronage plum when Hayes became President.

The new chief executive did not care for Conkling, nor did he intend to support the boss's cronies, so a battle for control of the customhouse ensued. Hayes abruptly dismissed Arthur and Cornell and appointed new officers, including Theodore Roosevelt, Sr., in their stead. Then he asked for Senate confirmation. Senator Conkling bitterly denounced the President and stoutly defended the tradition of senatorial courtesy. Hayes had certainly not consulted him about the change. The Senate ultimately refused to approve the new officers, no doubt realizing that if the President could successfully bypass so powerful a boss in the distribution of federal spoils in his state, any other politician might suffer a similar fate. Momentarily thwarted, Hayes bided his time; eventually he appointed other officers after the Senate had adjourned. Civil-service reform advocates in the Republican party applauded these forthright actions, even though the major effect was simply to return control of some of the spoils to the President.

Conkling's machine had thrived in proportion to its ability to guarantee federal jobs to its supporters. It was during this period that Conkling and his supporters had become known as Stalwarts, firmly loyal to Grant and the principles the party had developed during Reconstruction. Hayes had interfered drastically with the functioning of the New York Stalwart machine when he removed Arthur and Cornell. Oddly enough, both ousted men did quite well for themselves in the future. Arthur soon became President, and Cornell moved ahead in New York State politics. The Empire State had switched to a three-year gubernatorial term in 1876, which meant that the next election came around in 1879. The Stalwarts intended to rebuke the President by placing Cornell in the executive mansion at Albany in that year. Thus, through a process typical of boss-dominated politics, the state convention nominated Cornell for the governorship.

The New York Republican party by that time was divided into factions aligned with those outside the state. The Stalwarts' regular-party opponents, whom they derisively labeled "Half-Breeds," generally adopted a more pragmatic attitude toward the issues and hoped to create a new national Republican party to replace the one the Stalwarts favored, in which Northern moral attitudes prevailed. They also planned to take the patronage away from the Stalwarts at the earliest opportunity. Once the Stalwarts had captured the gubernatorial nomination for Cornell, however, the Half-Breeds grudgingly went along with the choice they had been unable to prevent. Party loyalty prevailed, giving the nominee a good start on the road to victory.

A third, much smaller faction in national politics was composed of Republican reformers who refused to support machine candidates. To distinguish themselves from both the Stalwarts and the Half-Breeds, these men called themselves Independent Republicans. Many of the Independents were former Liberal Republicans who had come back to the regular party's fold. The label came to apply generally to any member of the Republican party who was not associated with a particular machine or faction, and who was consequently opposed to patronage abuses. The New York Independents had praised Hayes' actions in ousting Cornell from the customhouse, and they had no intention of elevating the Stalwart leader to an even more influential position as governor of the state. On election day they turned in printed ballots listing the Republican party's slate of candidates for all state offices after having carefully scratched off the name of the Stalwart gubernatorial aspirant. This tactic earned them the popular nickname of Scratchers. The opposition candidate stood to benefit from this action on the part of the Independent Republicans but, unfortunately, the Democrats suffered a division in their own ranks. Tammany Hall boss John Kelly refused to support his party's regularly nominated candidate. As a result, his entire machine scratched their ballots as well. Cornell won the governorship through the good fortune of a more significant rebellion in the opposition party than had occurred in his own.

The scratching of tickets on both sides had important consequences. The Democrats recognized the power of the Tammany machine, and, during the next few years, the party's statewide leadership worked to heal the rift. When the next gubernatorial race rolled around, in 1882, the New York Democrats presented a united front. In one sense, the Republican Scratchers posed a more serious threat to party government than had the Democratic malcontents. The Tammany Braves who refused en masse to support the regular party choice merely illustrated the power inherent in a disciplined machine. The Independent Republicans called into question the soundness of the established party structures. Furthermore, the Scratchers had set a precedent for independent action. In refusing to vote for Cornell, the disgruntled reformers had obtained a hearing for their objections. They intended to use this publicity and the threat of another revolt at the upcoming 1880 national convention.

By 1880, the parties scarcely differed in their attitudes toward issues; they competed against each other simply to win political offices. Simultaneously, the reform concept had become a clearly defined national impulse, with both Republicans and Democrats taking cognizance of it. The reform movement had begun its rise in the Republican party, which had monopolized the federal patronage for two decades. Undisputed Republican control had enabled the party to perpetuate patronage abuses that had engendered dismay among the moralists in the party. The Democrats may have lacked the idealistic drive of the Independent Republican protesters, but they clearly perceived the popularity of the issue. Consequently, as it had done in 1872 and in 1876, the national Democratic platform in 1880 endorsed the principle of civil-service reform. The heart of the movement remained in the Republican party, however, were President Hayes' confusing attitudes toward reform encouraged the Independents to urge their party to take an unambiguous stand at the convention. Although the reform element remained a minority within it, the national Republican party included a full discussion of reform sentiments in its platform. Neither platform constituted a clear call for action, but both parties did officially recognize the public interest in reform.

Few expressed regret when Hayes announced that he would not seek renomination. The Independents hoped to prevent both Stalwart Grant and Half-Breed Blaine from snatching the nomination. At the same time, the beating he had just endured from Hayes put Roscoe Conkling in no mood to have his man turned aside again. At the convention he was breathing fire, intending to bring Grant back to the Presidency despite all obstacles. Treasury Secretary Sherman's manipulation of the spoils assured him third place in the balloting, while many Independents sponsored Senator George F. Edmunds of Vermont. The full convention conducted thirty-four almost identical roll-call ballots before some of the delegates began a stampede toward James A. Garfield, a noncontroversial Ohio statesman. Although the Independents accepted Garfield, who had been a Union general,

Conkling remained adamant to the end, and the solid bloc of 306 Stalwart votes he controlled frightened the other delegates into nominating ex-collector Chester A. Arthur for Vice-President. Conkling did not particularly appreciate this bone thrown in his direction, but he eventually did some perfunctory campaigning for the party's ticket.

A very close race ensued between Garfield and the Democratic nominee, another Civil War hero, named Winfield Scott Hancock. Even though General Hancock demonstrated almost total ignorance on political questions, he very nearly won, giving some indication of how unimportant some Americans considered the actual capabilities of their national leaders. The Independents, who had been gratified by Hayes' selection of Schurz, awaited Garfield's cabinet choices expectantly. The reformers lost all hope, however, when they learned that Blaine would be secretary of state. This appointment suggested that Garfield would rely heavily upon the Half-Breed faction and its machines. The rest of the cabinet did not please the Independents either, and it thoroughly incensed Stalwart Conkling. Giving the knife a final twist, President Garfield appointed yet another set of officers for the New York Customhouse without consulting Conkling, and the Stalwart boss completely lost his head. After the Senate reluctantly approved Garfield's appointments, Conkling resigned, along with his Stalwart subordinate, Senator Thomas C. Platt. He intended to have the New York legislature reappoint both of them to prove the strength of the Stalwart machine in his state. But the legislature ultimately refused to do Conkling's bidding, thereby forcing him into premature retirement from politics—but not before the factional warfare had produced its most unexpected casualty.

Charles Guiteau, an obviously insane man who claimed to be a Stalwart, shot and mortally wounded President Garfield on June 2, 1881. Letters found in the assassin's possession indicated that intense devotion to the Stalwart cause had motivated his deed. His action would eventually make Stalwart leader Chester Arthur President, to almost everyone's dismay. While the wounded President languished on his death bed, the Independent Republicans sprang into action. In July, they created the National Civil Service Reform League out of the crumbling foundations of the

New York Civil Service Reform Association, founded in 1877. They also began a concerted effort to convince the people that Garfield had been a victim of the spoils system. Upon the President's death in mid-September, the reformers claimed Garfield as a martyr. Whether or not he would have done much for their proposals had he lived, the dead President effectively symbolized the crucial need for some kind of reform.

Having given lip-service to reform proposals for years, both parties were now more or less committed to taking some action. If nothing else, they wished to silence the persistent Independent criticism. Since President Arthur's reputation and background made him an unsuitable spokesman for reform, Congress took the lead. The reform program had a dedicated advocate in Senator George Pendleton of Ohio. A Democrat from the state that bred Republican Presidents, Pendleton had become his party's leading proponent of civil-service reform. While he and other reformers agitated in the halls of Congress, outside events helped improve congressional receptivity to the reform suggestions. A minor economic recession hit the nation in the early 1880's, which somewhat eroded the people's faith in their Republican leaders. Simultaneously, bitter factional struggles weakened the Grand Old Party's position in the face of the rising power of the Democrats. Democratic candidates won decisively in several key elections in 1882. Although the Republicans managed to preserve an edge in the Senate, Democrats would outnumber them almost two to one in the upcoming House. This setback endangered Republican control of federal spoils.

The lame-duck session of the Republican-controlled Forty-Seventh Congress convened in December, 1882, and decided to take defensive measures. Fully aware of the Republican defeat, the congressmen hastily acted on virtually the only noteworthy bills of the decade, a controversial tariff revision act and the Pendleton Civil Service Act. Their motives were understandably mixed. Many of the Republicans voted in favor of the civil-service-reform bill because its tenure provisions would protect Republican partisans already in office; otherwise, the Democrats would turn them out if they won the Presidency in 1884. The Garfield tragedy influenced others, and some, of course, were sincerely dedicated to reform for its own sake. The precedent-setting action was hardly surprising, however; reformers had been laying the groundwork for it over the previous decade.

A New Yorker, Dorman B. Eaton, had actually written the Pendleton Bill. Eaton had been a consistent worker in reform circles over the years, and his proposed program proved highly acceptable to the Independent Republicans as well as others involved in the reform associations. A number of Democrats joined the bill's sponsor in voting for it, although some testily claimed that it would hoodwink them out of their natural rights to spoils. The bill won approval with a 38-to-5 Senate vote and a House majority of 155 to 47. President Arthur, who had risen to power through the sort of patronage abuses the Pendleton Bill was designed to wipe out, unhesitatingly signed it into law.

The Pendleton Civil Service Reform Act of January 16, 1883, empowered the President to appoint, with Senate approval, a three-man civil-service commission. The commissioners were charged with establishing a set of rules governing the appointment of certain types of federal employees. The bill spelled out in detail what these rules should do. The core of the system was to be "open, competitive examinations for testing the fitness of applicants for the public service." Offices would then be filled by selection from among those receiving the highest grades on the examinations. In addition, appointments were to be apportioned among the states on the basis of population. Officeholders already in service would have to take the examinations before they could win promotion.

The act stipulated several restrictions and guidelines as well. Once a man had received his appointment he would serve a period of probation. Habitual drunks were to be denied appointment, and nepotism involving more than two members of the same family was prohibited. Veterans were guaranteed a continuance of the preferential treatment already outlined in the United States statutes. To administer the examinations, the commission was to establish at least one board of examiners in every state, and select a chief examiner as well. Examinations would be offered twice a year.

Having outlined the operation desired in the reformed system, the act concluded with some provisions designed to protect it. A key point was the statement that congressmen's recommendations of applicants for the offices covered by the system should receive no consideration whatever in the appointment process. To insulate officers from political persuasion, the act forbid the solicitation of funds from federal officeholders.

The Pendleton Act indicated specifically which offices the system was intended to cover. If more than fifty employees worked in a Treasury tax-collecting facility or a post office, they were to be classified into ranks. The same classification system would be established in the cabinet departments in Washington. Those wishing to work in any of these classified positions had to pass the appropriate examinations. Because the great majority of the 100,000 federal officeholders worked in offices or bureaus employing fewer than fifty workers, only about 15 per cent of them would be covered by the new rules. Nevertheless, the most profitable elements of the spoils system, including, for example, the New York Customhouse, would fall under the merit system rules.

A provision authorizing the President to expand the number and character of offices classified pleased the reformers least for it implicitly empowered him to remove or exempt offices as well. The President thus could give the system a decent trial, or he could arbitrarily dissolve it. Arthur was hardly the President the reformers would have chosen but he did implement the Pendleton Act in a conscientious manner. He even selected Dorman Eaton, author of the bill, to be the first head of the Civil Service Commission. The commission applied merit rules promptly, and Arthur did not inhibit their effectiveness in any way. The chief executive's legal authority over the system remained unlimited, however, and not a few reformers worried about what the next President might do.

The Pendleton Act had consequences throughout the nation. Similar state civil-service-reform acts quickly appeared. The implementation of the Pendleton Act and its progeny represented a major step in the direction of a completely reformed civil-service system. Until the pattern of past practices had been broken, no over-all improvement could be expected. If nothing else, the federal action put some legislation on the books that detailed steps for the operation of the federal bureaucracy. This alone ensured further debate and discussion.

The passage of the Pendleton Act also greatly encouraged the advocates of reform. Having begun to alter the federal spoils system, the reformers drove ahead at the national level rather than contenting themselves with changes at the state level. The Independent Republicans had been willing to accept compromise Presidential candidates from the Republican party in the two previous national conventions, but now they would be more insistent that ever on having a voice in the nominations. The campaign and election of 1884 represented the apogee of reform activity. Some of those who participated in the exhilarating Mugwump movement in that year had long been involved in the reform struggle, but many new faces appeared in the ranks during the fascinating election campaign.

4. The Reformers

A party is only an instrument for creating and sustaining government. When it works for bad government and not for good, it is not only the right, but the duty, of every patriotic man to drop it and choose a better instrument.

—From an editorial published in the *New York Times*, June 26, 1884

The civil-service reformers of the Gilded Age were clearly bucking a leading political trend of their time in fighting the growth of machines. Depending heavily upon the operations of the spoils system, the powerful party organizations were increasingly intolerant of detractors. Consequently, the number of converts to reform and the singleness of purpose that eventually caused them to break their ties with the Republican party are surprising. The reform movement was not confined strictly to the Republican party, of course. Many Democrats—notably Samuel Tilden—took exception to the corrupt practices of the bosses who operated under the Democratic party label. Some of the most glaring patronage abuses occurred in the Republican party, however, for it had controlled federal spoils for years. Consequently, the

Republican reformers who questioned their own party's behavior attracted a good deal of attention.

As the Republican party was young, many of the impulses that had created it were still vibrant, just as many of the party's charter members were alive and active. A good part of the early Republican party's drive had emanated from zealous abolitionists, some of whom were committed to their ideal so fervently that they would risk destroying the Union rather than permit it to continue harboring the cancer of slavery. Appeals to exalted moral principles had characterized Republican oratory from the beginning, and many spokesmen considered their party a paragon of political virtue. To them, the compromising Democratic party appeared to be interested primarily in preserving itself, even at the cost of ignoring humanitarian principles. The power that the Republican party gained during the Civil War and seized and rationalized during Reconstruction helped it to implement its programs. But the party's success also attracted or promoted less scrupulous, less dedicated men to positions of power. Radical idealism gave way to Stalwart expediency and graft. The old zealots clung to the party out of hope, inertia, or fear that the opposition would be even worse. Gradually, however, as idealistic abolitionists had once risen to attack the Southern slavocracy, idealistic civil-service reformers rose to criticize what they considered the cause of poor government.

Had the Democrats appeared to be sincerely bent on self-purification, many of the reformers might have switched allegiance. Instead, the reviving Democratic party seemed willing to try almost any tactic, however questionable, to gain control of government offices. In desperation, the reformers became Liberal Republicans and tried to form an honorable third alternative. After the failure of that attempt in 1872, the reformers drifted back into the regular Republican party, which at least had once appealed to principles. Under Hayes, they could perceive some progress: the Conkling machine fell, and Secretary of the Interior Schurz established a model of reform in his department. With renewed hope, the idealists impatiently rode out the Stalwart–Half-Breed struggles. The Pendleton Act represented a long-sought prize, but the reformers worried that a new President might weaken or destroy this tentative first step, and they anxiously awaited the Presidential campaign of 1884. The historical association of moralists with the Republican party provides part of the explanation for the existence of Republican reformers in the late nineteenth century.

Richard Hofstadter has suggested that the reform movement developed inevitably as a consequence of a fundamental restructuring of the social system. Many of the reformers belonged to aristocratic New England families, and they quite naturally felt uncomfortable and resentful as coarser types began to displace them as the nation's social and political elite. Many of the leading Independent Republicans had inherited wealth, which imbued them with a somewhat more fastidious outlook than was typical of those who worked for their fortunes. Many of them had undergone classical educations, such as Harvard College offered. As gentlemen, distinguished from the commoner elements of society since birth, they may have felt they had a hereditary right to manage the affairs of state. They were shocked to discover that changes in the nation's power structure had altered their position in society and government—that a low-bred machine boss could create and hold political power by working hard at the grassroots level and, worse still, that the *nouveau riche* class could simply purchase power by making appropriate contributions to a political party. The displaced remnants of the erstwhile leadership became reformers in an attempt to limit and, they hoped, reverse this usurpation of their hereditary influence. A similar revolution had been occurring in American history ever since the first extensions of the franchise, however, so one must examine additional factors to understand fully how the reform class came into being.

Another historian, Gerald McFarland, culled from New York newspapers the names of some 400 prominent men who rebelled from the Republican party in 1884. He checked into each man's background and then was able to draw some general conclusions regarding the attributes these reformers shared. He discovered, for instance, that his rebels came almost wholly from the professional and managerial classes. A large proportion were businessmen or lawyers, and the rest included professors, doctors, and journalists. A substantial number were millionaires. Possessing prominence in nonpolitical fields, these reform leaders probably felt an obligation to step in and right political wrongs.

Another historian, Ari Hoogenboom, contends that political ambition was a major factor behind Independent Republican behavior. Many of those who became reformers had failed to achieve political prominence within the existing system, which was falling under machine domination, and so determined to overthrow that system and champion a new one. If they succeeded in abolishing the spoils system upon which the machines thrived, they felt that they would become natural candidates for high office. Hoogenboom's explanation fits at least those reformers who participated actively in party affairs. Indeed, many of the professional politicians who considered themselves reformers steadfastly remained loyal to their party, thereby protecting their own political futures. A good many others, however, were not so motivated, having a less than professional interest in politics and a more serious concern about good government.

It appears that the Republican party's traditional reputation for moralism ensured the continued affiliation of idealists appalled by the antics of cruder partisans. Some of the critics probably felt that the machines had cheated them out of their divine right to rule. Others seemed to feel a moral responsibility to cleanse the political soul of the nation. Still others obviously hoped that, by reforming the parties, they could obtain the positions currently monopolized by machine partisans. In view of these diverse motivations, it was not surprising that a parting of the ways occurred in 1884, with some of the reformers remaining loyal to the party and others deciding that continued support would be incompatible with their principles.

While Republican idealists kept the reform concept alive within their party, pragmatic men were exploiting it for their own purposes. Some of them were gambling that the reformers would win in the long run; others merely hoped to ride with the popular issue until another came along. The more interest the reform issue attracted, the more adherents it gathered, particularly as long as they could continue operating within the standard Republican framework. These less principled individuals tended to dilute the dedication of the reform movement. The idealists, who often regarded themselves as the only decent members of their party, accepted support from others who intended to use the movement's popularity to their own advantage. The fellow travelers of the reform impulse suffered a shock in the late spring of 1884, when a substantial group of reformers left the regular party. At that point a clear split developed between those who considered reform essential at all cost and those who did not wish to jeopardize their careers within the party.

The politicians who were building and strengthening party organizations were keeping up with the times. They were, in fact, among the most forward-looking elements in the political system, for they were following the national trends toward order, combination, and coordination, prevalent in so many other endeavors. Whatever else can be said about the reformers of the 1870's and 1880's, they were out of step with these trends. When the reform movement challenged the machines, the bosses not only countered it but succeeded in further entrenching their control.

The reform movement's self-righteous criticism of the bosses for stealing political power from the people and consolidating it for their own use had its ironic aspects. In fact, the reformers were not proponents of democracy in the sense that they believed in social and political equality. Although they may have favored extension of the franchise, when it came to operating the government, the reformers were interested in seeing to it that only "qualified" men should take office. Their goal of removing all but the most scrupulously honest bureaucrats and protecting them totally from outside persuasion might have created a government less responsive to the popular will than the one currently in existence. If nothing else, political machines provided a means for those with special interests to influence political and government action.

The reformers hoped to use a revolutionary plan, a merit system for the civil service, to perform the basically reactionary function of returning control of the government to society's natural aristocrats. They seemed intent upon restoring the system of government the Founding Fathers had favored, in which educated, skilled, and presumably impartial men would rule the nation for the benefit of all. In its original form, the Constitution carefully insulated parts of the government from the people. The most obvious example is the electoral college, which filtered the people's Presidential choices through a group of supposedly responsible men. In 1787 some upper-class Americans had drafted a plan of government which would keep government power in their hands. In a sense, the reformers were only trying to revert to that earlier system.

Certain critics of the reform movement were well aware of these motivations on the part of the reformers. These opponents of the merit system complained that only highly educated men could pass the proposed civil-service examinations. Self-made Westerners felt that they could not successfully compete for jobs with college-trained Easterners. Although the reformers disavowed any intention of cutting lower-class men as a group out of government service, the examination system would probably do just that. An educated elite could eventually dominate a federal bureaucracy based completely upon merit and could exercise a conservative and rational control over its operations. Discrimination through superior education would keep the common man out of power as effectively in the 1880's as it does today a member of a ghetto-bred minority. A reformed civil service would not necessarily serve the people as a whole. Instead, it might become the pawn of the educated class, a small and nonrepresentative portion of the nation's population.

The geographic profile of the reform movement betrayed its parochial nature. Reform sentiment flourished in New York and Massachusetts, with pockets in Connecticut and other New England states as well. Now and then a reformer made a name for himself in the West, as did William Dudley Foulke in Indiana, but in general regionalism characterized the movement. If they could wipe out machine control at the national level, the self-appointed advocates of reform might possibly take full command of their party. Many Easterners considered this a major goal. Theodore Roosevelt and Henry Cabot Lodge both favored an educated, elitist bureaucracy which would, in the British pattern, conduct brilliant foreign policies without fear of partisan removal.

The leading reformer in the nation was George William Curtis, who had been closely associated with Ralph Waldo Emerson and the Transcendental Movement in New England. After spending two years at Brook Farm, where his idealism and concern for his fellowman were strengthened, Curtis published, in the early 1850's, books of social commentary and travel notes that established his literary reputation. He subsequently became even more famous as an orator, and his patriotic exhortations during the Civil War found appreciative audiences.

Urbane and industrious, Curtis pursued a career related to but outside of politics, depending upon his literary skill to support him rather than on government or party positions. He became editor of *Harper's Weekly* in 1863, a position he held for most of his remaining working career. Under his supervision, *Harper's* became a popular magazine with nationwide circulation. It combined political editorials with literature, commentary, and political cartoons. *Harper's* had been a crusading abolitionist journal before the war, and when Curtis took over it continued along the same lines, criticizing the Southern rebellion and praising emancipation and Radical Reconstruction schemes. After the war, the magazine continued to try to influence public opinion, and it had helped to publicize such injustices as the operations of the Tweed Ring. As long as Curtis remained in charge, the weekly served as a leading reform journal, with the full approval of its publishers, the Harper brothers.

While not financially dependent upon politics, Curtis was nevertheless deeply involved. He had been a Republican since the party was formed. He perennially served as a Republican delegate to both state and national conventions, representing New York at the convention that nominated Lincoln in 1860. He once had political ambitions, but after losing a bid for the New York gubernatorial nomination in 1870, he became less partisan and more critical of his party's operations. As a party regular and a supporter of Radical programs, Curtis knew and respected Ulysses Grant. His connections with the President led to Grant's appointing Curtis chairman of the short-lived civil service commission formed in the early 1870's and prevented the reform editor from joining the Liberal Republican revolt. Curtis helped to found the New York Civil Service Association and later served as its president. This experience earned him the presidency of the

National Civil Service Reform League, which was founded shortly after Garfield's assassination. Under Curtis's management the League published pamphlets and sponsored investigations and reports relating to civil-service abuses. After the Pendleton Act had won approval, the league served as a watchdog over the progress of its implementation. Curtis circulated at the highest levels in New York society, and his personal associates both inside and outside the reform movement clearly belonged to an aristocratic elite. As an experienced and respected reform crusader, Curtis would play a large role in the campaign of 1884. Until then, he remained a member in good standing of the Republican party, a position that offered him great opportunities and saddled him with great responsibilities.

A reformer deeply enmeshed in the affairs of the Republican party was Carl Schurz. Unlike Curtis, he had no permanent source of outside income and was, therefore, more interested in making a living at politics. After leaving Germany, Schurz became known in the United States for his journalistic and forensic talents. He served in the Union army and emerged from the war with the rank of major-general, a valuable asset for any politician. As a Radical Republican Senator from Missouri, Schurz apparently threw away all chance of further advancement when he led the Liberal Republican sortie from the party in 1872. Surprisingly, he bounced back again to serve in Hayes' cabinet until 1881. Between 1881 and 1884, Schurz remained pretty much at loose ends. For a brief period he served as one of a triumvirate of editors for the *New York Evening Post*, but personal conflicts with another editor, E. L. Godkin, caused him to resign. He remained jobless through the election of 1884, a circumstance that may have been financially unsettling, but left him completely free to devote his considerable talents to reform agitation. Indeed, of all the reformers who broke with the Republican party in 1884, Schurz expended the most effort speaking everywhere and rousing rebel sentiments. Schurz would remain a major force in politics through the end of the century and eventually replaced Curtis as editor of *Harper's Weekly*.

Some men managed to become almost professional civil-service reformers. Dorman B. Eaton shares with Curtis and Schurz the chief responsibility for the establishment of the merit system in the federal government. A graduate of the University of Vermont and the Harvard Law School, Eaton practiced law until 1870, after which he devoted all his time to the reform movement. President Grant chose Eaton to succeed Curtis as civil service commissioner in 1873. That position disappeared when Congress refused to appropriate funds for it, and President Hayes then had Eaton make a study of the British civil service system, which was published in 1880. As the recognized American expert on the subject, Eaton was the logical choice to draft the bill that became the Pendleton Act and to serve once again as civil service commissioner. When he eventually retired from that position, he turned his attention to the reform of municipal government, particularly in New York City.

One of Eaton's fellow New Yorkers whose career benefited much from his reform activities was Silas W. Burt. The holder of a civil engineering degree from Union College, Burt served as assistant inspector general for the state of New York during the Civil War. He became the first examiner of the federal civil service commission in 1871, and he helped found and later became president of the Civil Service Reform Association of New York. Through the 1870's he worked at the New York Customhouse, eventually becoming President Hayes' choice to replace Alonzo Cornell as Naval Officer. After President Arthur ousted Burt from the Customhouse in 1883, Democratic Governor Grover Cleveland arranged for the reformer to become chief examiner for the New York Civil Service Commission. When he became President, Cleveland returned Burt to his old New York Customhouse post. In the 1890's Burt headed the New York Civil Service Commission. Burt was recognized as a leading reformer and expert in civil service matters, and he cooperated with reformers both inside and outside government positions.

Journalistic skill was a common characteristic among the Independent Republican reformers. Outspoken Edwin Lawrence Godkin edited two reform publications, the daily *New York Evening Post* and a weekly, the *Nation*. Especially after Schurz left the *Post* in 1882, Godkin made the *Nation* into a sort of weekly summary of the daily paper's commentaries. Ultimately, the *Nation* became the leading weekly journal of political opinion. Standing somewhat outside the mainstream of American politics, the Irish-born Godkin could dispassionately judge and assess political questions. For thirty-five years, he exerted a persuasive influence upon national thinking, advocating political reforms of all kinds and acting as a leading propagandist for civil-service reform.

Whereas Godkin was a journalist uninterested in politics for personal advancement, other members of the reform group had serious political ambitions. This wing of the Independent Republican faction included Senator George F. Hoar of Massachusetts. Hoar, a graduate of Harvard College and Harvard Law School, made his start in politics by assisting his father, Samuel Hoar, and his brother, Ebenezer Rockwood Hoar, in organizing the Free-Soil party in Massachusetts. He then took the short step from the Free-Soil to the Republican party, which sent him to the state legislature in 1852. He served in Congress from 1869 until 1877, when he was elected to a seat in the Senate, which he held until his death in 1904.

Unlike many of his political contemporaries, Hoar never became wealthy, living frugally on his salary and the proceeds of a small law practice. His prewar idealism made him a natural advocate of postwar reform, and the Senator carried on a pugnacious campaign for his principles. Not dependent for support upon machines in his own bailiwick, Hoar worked persistently to root out machines in other areas. His brother Ebenezer, a distinguished lawyer and Attorney General under Grant, had suffered badly at the hands of the bosses. Grant had nominated Judge Hoar to fill the vacant chief justice's seat on the Supreme Court, but the appointment had failed in the Senate, a victim of factionalism. Thus, Senator Hoar had personal as well as moral reasons for supporting the reform movement.

A younger Massachusetts politician, Henry Cabot Lodge, became a reformer for many of the same reasons as Hoar. Scion of a socially eminent Boston dynasty, Lodge possessed the Harvard education, social graces, and native intelligence necessary to make him a favorite among the Boston Brahmins. He, too, had not exploited machine connections to get ahead, and he was more than willing to ennoble the political profession he had chosen to pursue by ousting undesirable types. A state legislator in the early 1880's and very active in local party affairs, Lodge was a well-placed spokesman for reform.

Another Harvard-educated reformer just beginning to make a reputation for himself was young Theodore Roosevelt. President Hayes had appointed Roosevelt's father, an irreproachably honest man, to replace one of Conkling's henchmen in the New York Customhouse battle in 1878, so young Teedee, as he was then called, came by his principles naturally. Soon after his graduation from Harvard in 1880, he had won election to the New York legislature. To do so, Roosevelt had to join a local Republican club, which gave him his assembly nomination and helped him win the election. Once in Albany, Assemblyman Roosevelt led the reform charge. With the Pendleton Act as a guide, Roosevelt saw to it that New York State adopted a merit system of her own. Roosevelt had already clearly identified his interests with those of the reformers as the party prepared for the 1884 battle.

Political ambition took some bizarre forms, however, as the example of the Reverend Henry Ward Beecher shows. Before the Civil War, Beecher had become closely identified with the extreme abolitionists. His well-publicized assistance to and encouragement of antislavery settlers in Kansas had played no small part in stimulating bloody strife in that area. Idealism and an often fanatical espousal of principles characterized the minister's every public action. He thus appeared to be a classic example of the abolition-idealist turned civil-service-reform zealot. In 1884 Beecher vociferously supported reform policies prior to the Republican national convention. The reformers intended to create a stalemate between supporters of President Arthur and James Blaine. Beecher hoped that the stalemate would break in his favor. Thus political ambition played a large part in his reform fulminations.

Youth was not unusual among the reformers. Roosevelt was only 25 in the spring of 1884, and the reform issue appealed to many men who had only recently become involved in party politics. In part, they favored reform because it gave clear signs of future success. The passage of the Pendleton Act had reinforced this conviction, for it appeared to be one of the most significant changes made in the governing process of the United States since the war. If they were not already members of machines, young partisans found the reform movement consistent with their youthful idealism. Among the prominent young Massachusetts men who rebelled from the Republican party in 1884 was John Andrew, son of his state's wartime Republican governor. As the possessor of a famous name, John Andrew had reason to expect a successful career in his father's party, but he eventually decided that reform ideas were more compelling than party ties. A few Republican reformers, including Andrew, became so disgusted with their party's tactics that they subsequently became full-fledged Democrats.

Another young Bostonian, Moorfield Storey, possessed the Harvard degree essential for admission to the city's elite social circles. Born too late to participate in the Civil War, Storey left the Harvard Law School to serve under Radical Senator Charles Sumner in his position as chairman of the Senate Committee on Foreign Relations. He returned to Boston in 1869 and from then on pursued an extraordinarily successful career as a business lawyer. In his political endeavors, however, Storey insisted upon advocating a number of relatively unpopular, idealistic programs. He played an important role in the Massachusetts reform movement and typified the wealthy, socially prominent reform activists in New England.

A famous reformer out of the mainstream of politics was Thomas Wentworth Higginson. A descendant of the Massachusetts Bay Colony's first minister, Higginson was graduated from Harvard in 1841 at the age of seventeen, only to return and take a divinity degree six years later. As one of the most radical abolitionists in the nation, the young minister had gone so far as to advocate disunion in the 1850's. He traveled to Bleeding Kansas in 1856 and became acquainted with John Brown, whom Higginson later supported and defended. When the Civil War broke out, Higginson volunteered for service and was honored by being named colonel of the first black regiment in the Union Army. After the war, Higginson devoted his attention to writing. He never ceased his advocacy of reforms of all sorts, including temperance, women's rights, and, inevitably a merit civil-service system. He served a term as a Massachusetts legislator in the early 1880's but his primary contributions to the reform cause stemmed from his literary endeavors.

Young reformers might be interested either in furthering their political careers or in participating in a socially acceptable endeavor. The older men attracted to reform might also be primarily concerned over their own political prospects, but many of the reformers were, like Higginson, simply idealists who sincerely felt that the nation's government was falling into the hands of men lacking in honesty or a sense of justice. Curtis and Godkin, secure in their editorial positions, appear to have been motivated almost exclusively by such high principles. Besides, many of the leading reformers valued themselves so highly that they would have refused almost any government job offered them short of a cabinet post. Making a virtue out of necessity, most reformers repeatedly stressed their disinterest in political advancement and their concern only for the betterment of government and society.

The reform movement never grew large in absolute numbers, but the prestige of its individual members gave it an inordinate amount of influence. The dedicated reformers who acted as mainstays in the various reform clubs represented only a small minority of the Republican party. Although they controlled a sizable share of the New York City press, they were unable to do more than act as a swing force. Fortunately, as long as the Republican party remained split between the supporters of Grant and Blaine, Independent Republicans had been able to capitalize on their independence. The reiteration of reform principles in succeeding Republican platforms indicates that the movement's philosophy exercised a good bit of influence in party councils. The relatively small size of the reform wing coupled with its idealism made it an unorthodox political force. Constantly criticizing the machines, yet needing machine support or at least a machine-induced stalemate in order to gain a hearing, the Independent Republicans led a precarious existence. They eventually came to consider the 1884 Presidential race a crucial test of their whole political philosophy. Their sometimes heroic and often absurd actions during the race showed both the strengths and weaknesses of their cause, of the predominant political parties, and of the nation itself.

PART II

The Attack on Party
Organizations in 1884

5. The Republican Organization

The Republican Party could nominate a wooden Indian cigar store sign for President, and elect it.

—Attributed to Republican Senator JOSEPH HAWLEY of Connecticut by the *New York World*, May 29, 1884

Like the regular Republicans, the Independents realized that the 1884 race would be quite different from the previous two, now that the Stalwart faction had deteriorated. In the national conventions of 1876 and 1880, the Stalwarts had insisted on sponsoring a third term for Grant, even though the former President had alienated many party members by his unspectacular leadership. The pro-Grant wing of the party possessed a large enough minority of the convention votes to prevent Half-Breed James G. Blaine from capturing the nomination. But the stalemate Grant's candidacy had produced in 1876 and 1880 would not recur in 1884. Conkling's solid phalanx of Stalwarts had broken up. Some would swing behind Chester Arthur, some would support local favorite sons, but the Independent Republicans had to acknowledge glumly that many of Grant's former advocates would just as surely turn to Blaine. And the civil-service reformers had developed an almost pathological distrust of the Half-Breed faction's chieftain.

The Independents' anti-Blaine campaign of 1884 illustrates the irrationality that often accompanies an emotional crusade. The reformers started out with a reasonable complaint about the way political affairs were developing. They noted correctly that the existing party organizations seldom provided the kind of government that was desirable and necessary for the nation at that time. The merit system the reformers had helped to institute was not designed to force any particular individual out of political action, but they hoped it would destroy the self-seeking machines. Through their leagues and reform clubs, the Independents had developed a reputation for rational and intelligent action. They lost that and more in the 1884 campaign as they gradually turned into one-sided partisans, fulminating in an often undignified and emotional manner. Since they had predicated their efforts on moral principles, they ultimately felt justified in taking almost any kind of action. The Republican party's inevitable nomination of Blaine was the catalyst for this change from deliberate, sober action to frenzied campaigning.

An unemotional examination of the catalytic agent scarcely explains this frenetic reaction. James Gillespie Blaine was certainly one of the most widely respected Republican leaders in the country at the time. He had not earned the admiration that Grant, a successful general, received, but he also did not appear to be a corrupt political opportunist like Roscoe Conkling. Although Blaine had pursued his political career in Maine, he had roots in the nation's heartland. Born in western Pennsylvania in 1830, he had obtained what in those days passed for a thorough education. The youthful Blaine became a school teacher in Kentucky in 1848 and was married there shortly afterward. A few years later, he returned to Pennsylvania and in 1853 migrated to Maine, where he soon became a popular journalist. Journalism and politics went hand in hand in the nineteenth century, so by 1863 the transplanted teacher had become one of Maine's representatives in the United States Congress.

From that point on, Blaine's career resembled that of a typical,

if unusually successful, Gilded Age politician, except that he managed to avoid military service with the contention that his work
in the House would be a more valuable contribution to the war
effort than any he might make on the battlefield. Blaine threw
in his lot with the Radical Republicans, and by 1869 this association had made him speaker of the house, a position he held
until his admirers in Maine boosted him to the United States
Senate in 1876. After barely losing his party's nomination for the
Presidency in 1876, Blaine kept his name before the public
through his Senate activities. Again in 1880, he seemed almost
certain to advance to the White House until the Stalwarts refused to accede to his nomination and forced his supporters to
turn to Garfield. But Blaine's Half-Breed faction held a controlling interest in Garfield's administration, and the President acknowledged his debts by appointing Blaine secretary of state.

According to all accounts, Blaine thoroughly enjoyed his work
at the State Department. Having lost the Presidency twice, he
developed something of a superstition about the office, feeling
that he could never win it. After 1880, he seemed genuinely
reluctant to try again for the nation's top office, but his extraordinary popularity and obvious talents ensured his inevitable
reconsideration in the future. A term as secretary of state had
formerly been an almost certain pathway to the Presidency, and
Blaine hardly hid his light under a bushel. He actually served
only a few months, for Vice-President Arthur's succession upon
Garfield's death made him uncomfortable in the cabinet. The
Half-Breed leader could not countenance working under one of
the Stalwarts who had been reviling him for years.

Blaine did manage to make those few months memorable, if
not altogether admirable, in the annals of American foreign
relations. Diplomacy had received very little attention after 1871,
when Secretary of State Hamilton Fish had won a favorable
settlement of the United States Civil War claims against Great
Britain. Blaine brought foreign affairs back into public awareness,
although not always in the most commendable manner. He sent
incompetent ministers to Chile and Peru, who nearly involved
the United States directly in a border war between the two South
American countries. Blaine performed a more beneficial service

for the Western Hemisphere when he planned a meeting of Latin American leaders to discuss trade and amity. The invitations Blaine sent out were later withdrawn, but he eventually did host a Pan-American conference in 1890, after he had resumed control of the State Department under President Benjamin Harrison. Before he resigned from Arthur's cabinet in 1881, Blaine boosted his reputation as a spokesman for American rights in two matters concerning Great Britain. First he attempted to abrogate the Clayton-Bulwer Treaty of 1850, which forbade the building of American fortifications along the proposed Panama Canal, by appealing to the Monroe Doctrine and emphasizing the supremacy of the United States in the Western Hemisphere. Then he diplomatically intervened in some cases involving naturalized American citizens who had returned to their homes in Ireland and been arrested for treason by British authorities. Although neither action had much impact abroad, both reinforced Blaine's public image as a patriot.

After he left the cabinet, Blaine ostensibly retired to private life. He began writing a history of his congressional career, called *Twenty Years of Congress*. Sections of the work were printed from time to time and sent to subscribers, a common method of publishing in the nineteenth century. This process continually reminded the people of his existence and of his participation in national events during and after the Civil War. As the time approached for selecting a Republican nominee for the 1884 Presidential race, Blaine's name received constant mention. The pro-Grant opposition had broken, and Arthur's hastily assembled supporters seemed rather forlorn. One of the few obstacles in Blaine's way was his unpopularity with the Independent Republicans.

Personally, Blaine appears to have been about as honest as the average professional politician. He did not become fabulously wealthy, nor did he fail to prosper. Along with hundreds of others, he took advantage of the opportunities that came his way. Whether these opportunities led him to step outside strictly legal limits is debatable. His critics considered his actions immoral to a degree directly proportional to their own frames of reference. Industry, finance, and business were operating under a laissez-faire philosophy in the late nineteenth century, and politicians could hardly be expected to observe higher standards of behavior than the businessmen and entrepreneurs around them.

Blaine was popular, respected, and powerful. His supporters and his enemies alike acknowledged that he possessed an ample measure of "personal magnetism," which modern commentators would call charisma. A tall, commanding figure of a man, he could entrance audiences with his great oratorical skill. The words might be mundane or meaningless, but his delivery was magnificent. He also had the advantage of an unusually keen memory. Stopping at some wayside hamlet while touring the nation, he could immediately recognize men he had met only once many years earlier. Those who were thus flattered would remain his avid supporters for life. But, as is often the case with extremes, Blaine's extraordinary popularity triggered an equally intense dislike among certain groups. The more enthusiastic his following grew, the more suspicious his critics became. When Blaine finally began to praise the very reforms they advocated, the Independents refused to credit his sincerity, dismissing his remarks as another example of his political opportunism. They very likely were, but, being the adept politician he was, once Blaine had come out in favor of reform, he might well have followed through with more success than the estranged reform group could have achieved.

Nothing in the Blaine story just related would appear to make him unacceptable to the reformers. On the surface, he seemed no worse, if perhaps little better, than his whole generation of politicians. But the Independents were not concerned with surface manifestations; their opposition went much deeper. Blaine had used the very methods the reformers deplored in making his way to the top. He was one of the prime beneficiaries of the sort of party organizations that the Independent Republicans hoped to destroy. Ex-spoilsman Chester Arthur currently occupied the White House, but he was an accidental President, unexpectedly boosted into the office. The deliberate nomination of a man of Blaine's ilk, the Independents felt, would be inconsistent with the traditions of the party they honored.

In fact, corruption had not tainted Blaine nearly so much as it had many other political leaders. Although his position and influence in the party resembled those of a typical senate boss, he had not needed vast sums of money or an army of civil servants to maintain his eminence, for the state of Maine was perennially Republican and proud of it. Blaine made sure that he got his share of federal patronage to dole out to friends, but it served more as a prerogative of his office than as a necessity for retaining it. The reformers tended to ignore such extenuating circumstances. They simply lumped Blaine together with other representatives of the system they disliked. They knew that he would gratefully accept whatever assistance machines offered him, and they considered his friends and associates in the party responsible for debasing the whole system. Hayes and Garfield might not have been the most statesmanlike men ever nominated, but at least their relative obscurity absolved them of identification with the leading corruptors of the party.

Blaine's impartiality and integrity were open to serious question. As a thoroughgoing partisan, he considered his party's interests identical to those of the nation and thus he seemed willing to consort with any type of partisan to ensure a Republican victory. How much of Blaine's thinking represented self-delusion and how much simple political ambition will never be known. He obviously understood the tactics professional politicians employed, having survived and prospered in the cutthroat political system of the age. His successful participation in politics for so many years necessarily involved his condoning many questionable tactics, and it almost had to limit his ability to view them dispassionately. Reformers imbued with a moralistic fervor did not weigh political actions subjectively. They considered a particular action either honest or dishonest, and they could not support a man who might let expediency determine his behavior.

The recent passage of the Pendleton Act projected the whole reform movement into a new phase. Before the act's approval, the civil-service advocates had not considered a President's support of their reform schemes as crucial to their success. Neither Hayes nor Garfield had been avid reformers; nor had either man been a mindless machine functionary. But the Independent Republicans had never expected a President alone to change the system. They had been working through congressmen like Pendleton, Hoar, and Lodge, and, when Congress approved the merit program, the Independents decided that these tactics were effective. They grossly underestimated the impetus given to the Pendleton Bill by the incoming Democratic House as well as by the growing realization in both parties that skilled civil servants were essential. Nevertheless, the reformers inundated the nation with self-congratulatory statements in the wake of the bill's approval, and they chose to view the state programs patterned after it as further vindication of their reform sentiments. This very success posed implicit dangers, however, for it tended to make the Independent Republicans overconfident. Their endeavors had been fruitless for so long that they grossly inflated this relatively limited victory, praising it as only the first step toward the inevitable restructuring of the whole party system. The Pendleton Act also reinforced the reformers' convictions that they should concentrate their attention at the federal level, even though much of the machines' strength was at local levels.

The most significant change brought about by passage of the Pendleton Act was that the Independents now had something to lose. So long as they had made no palpable progress, they could continue agitating for reform without risking anything if reform did not come. They could remain inside the Republican party, decrying its corruption while awaiting future success. The Pendleton Act changed that. Many reformers felt that if they had to backtrack even slightly after their first victory, they might be totally discredited. The act had given the chief executive so much latitude in administering the civil-service rules that an unfriendly President could easily render them unworkable. Consequently, the selection of Arthur's successor became of utmost concern to the Independents. Whatever else he was, Blaine had never been a committed advocate of reform. Since the Independents refused to believe he could change his spots, they intended to prevent their nascent reform program from falling into his hands.

The reformers had difficulty in trying to imbue others with a distrust of Blaine, particularly when so many started out with basically positive attitudes toward him. In an attempt at conversion, his dedicated foes exposed and publicized what they considered a tangible manifestation of his baseness. The Mulligan letters provided the Independent Republicans with just enough substance to support their assertions.

In 1876, the Democrats controlled the House of Representatives, and they set up an investigating committee to look into the possibility that certain Republican congressmen might be involved in conflicts of interest. Blaine became one of the chief subjects of the investigation. James Mulligan, personal secretary to a railroad promoter named Warren Fisher, came forward with some correspondence that his boss had exchanged with Blaine. Fisher was president of the Fort Smith and Little Rock Railroad in 1869, while Blaine was serving as speaker of the house. At that time, a bill involving Fisher's railroad interests came up for consideration in the House. The letters Mulligan produced hinted that Blaine had used his influence as Speaker to prevent action adverse to the railroad's interests. In return, Blaine appeared to have asked for and received an especially generous deal in obtaining railroad stock.

The letters themselves became a bone of contention when Mulligan offered to present them to the committee. As Mulligan told the story, Blaine visited him one evening and pleaded to be given a chance to look over the correspondence. Mulligan finally agreed when the politician promised to return the letters to him. Instead, Blaine had marched into the House "like a Plumed Knight" and read the entire set of letters into the *Congressional Record*, adding his own interpretations and comments along the way. He claimed that he had been buying and selling bonds as a private citizen and had never allowed such personal dealings to influence his actions in Congress. The investigating committee subsequently failed to bring any charges against Blaine, and his devotees felt that he had totally exonerated himself. His flamboyant actions did not so easily convince his enemies.

The Mulligan incident took place in the spring of 1876, crucially timed for the upcoming Republican convention. It may have reduced Blaine's chances of winning the Presidential nomination, and a heat stroke he suffered later in the year limited them still further. Although he recovered fully from his illness, the nomination went to Hayes. Controversy over the Mulligan letters arose again in 1880, but this time it was the stubborn

Stalwart delegates who stymied his chances for the nomination. The letters had become a tired issue by 1884, and Blaine's popularity had not appreciably diminished in the eight years since their first revelation. The Independent Republicans who hoped to use this excuse to discredit Blaine were undertaking an uphill battle.

By reviving the old controversy, they intended to show that Blaine had been a corrupt, self-seeking politician. Although the 1876 investigation had proved inconclusive, Blaine's enemies wanted to believe the worst, and they felt that the Mulligan letters were only an example of many such bargains and deals Blaine had made. Blaine was doing fairly well financially in the 1880's, a usual circumstance for an astute politician in that or any age. He could have made his fortune honestly, carefully separating his private business transactions from his role as a public servant, but had he done so he would have been unique among politicians. Whatever his guilt or innocence, the Independents considered him too corrupt to merit the honor of the Republican party nomination. They had just celebrated the passage of the first legislation aimed at destroying the federal power base for political bosses. Blaine had been too influential too long in the old system to satisfy the Independents, who would consider his elevation to the Presidency as a disastrous step back toward the system they had been fighting for years.

The attitude of individual Independents toward Blaine ranged from mild distaste to blind hatred. They might consider the Mulligan letters an unfortunate lapse or a symbol of Blaine's complete corruption. Blaine's milder critics hoped that the convention would nominate someone else; although they viewed the prospect of Blaine's nomination with alarm, their party loyalty would restrain them from precipitous action. His most extreme and steadfast opponents would risk all to prevent him from becoming President; they preferred to leave the party rather than vote for a man they considered totally unworthy.

Most Independent Republicans were also appalled at the thought of another term for Chester Arthur, the only other serious contender for the Republican nomination. Arthur's undynamic leadership and his unsavory earlier connections with Conkling's

Stalwart apparatus made him as unappealing as Blaine. The Independents cast about for a champion of their own as an alternative. The possible choices turned out to be quite limited. None of the leading Independents had a real chance. Schurz was not native-born; Hoar was too irascible; Curtis was an editor, not a politician. Further, the very independence of these men meant that the party regulars would probably consider them unacceptable. The Independents' ultimate choice shows how desperate they were. Although they had no doubt about whom they did *not* want to be President, they could not be certain they had found the proper alternative in George F. Edmunds of Vermont.

Edmunds' candidacy did not burst afresh on the political scene in 1884. He had served in the Senate for years and had won a smattering of support at the Presidential nominating convention in 1880, when the Independents had earlier sought a safe recipient for their votes. Still, only someone who disliked the other candidates a good deal could consider the taciturn New Englander at all. Edmunds did not possess a spectacular record. Fortunately, he had only rarely associated with machines, for Vermont Republicans were so loyal to the party that organization was almost superfluous in that state. Representing a guaranteed constituency, Senator Edmunds had been able to behave exactly as he pleased. According to his Independent backers, he had voted "correctly" on nonpartisan issues, and his honesty and respectability had earned high praise. At the same time, he had remained thoroughly committed to the party; he had never opposed Grant, and he was not a reformer, an action that would have required more energy than he seemed willing to expend.

Thus Edmunds appears an odd candidate for the Independents to choose. His honesty and his lack of machine connections were praiseworthy, particularly when he was compared to Blaine in these respects. Yet his other qualifications were hardly superior. In the Senate, he had always devoted more attention to correct parliamentary and constitutional procedure than to the substance of the bills. He was neither dynamic nor charismatic. And by no means could he be called an avid reformer, although he would probably have responded to advocates of reform. He did possess one important advantage over any of the reformers: he was available. He might not generate much enthusiasm, but nothing in his past or present attitudes would frighten away any Republican. His unquestioned loyalty to the party would make him acceptable even to the machines. Because his career had been so undramatic, he had alienated no one. As the reformers' best hope, however, he showed their weakness and, in the end, he represented nothing more than a Hobson's choice.

Regardless of their attitudes before the convention, the Independent Republicans had little to lose by making their preferences known. They considered Blaine the chief enemy and early began considering how best to hurt his chances. As an amorphous group of protesters, their possibilities for action were somewhat limited. Fundamentally opposed to the overstructuring of the parties, they never considered forming a machine of their own. Organizing the Independent Republicans would prove difficult in any case. Their name truthfully implied a commitment to independence from the persuasions of party leaders and factions. Few intended to relinquish that independence even to a group of their own kind, unless that group's attitudes exactly matched their own. The voluntary political associations of Independents that did exist operated cautiously, unsure of the proper means to the ends they all desired. The Liberal Republican experience had taught them that an early exit from the regular party had serious drawbacks. Thus the Independents decided to remain associated with the party as long as possible and to devote their energies to wooing it away from Blaine. If they succeeded in denying him the nomination, the reformers would be in a powerful bargaining position when—and if—the party took office.

To make any impact in the campaign, the Independents first had to get the attention of the nation and of their fellow Republicans. To that end, the Young Men's Republican Club of Brooklyn, New York, invited a group of influential Republicans to a banquet on February 22, 1884. Carl Schurz and President Julius H. Seelye of Amherst College spoke at the dinner, setting the tone for the meeting. The Independent Republicans intended to make their principles clear early in the year so that the rest of the party would realize the advisability of nominating a man the reformers considered acceptable. Consequently, on the following day, they established an Independent Republican Committee to help publicize their sentiments and determination. A large, enthusiastic attendance at the banquet and subsequent organizational meeting demonstrated the strength and resolve that the Independent Republicans felt early in 1884.

A most significant aspect of the meeting was the attention it got in the newspapers. A political banquet on Washington's Birthday was hardly unusual, but the broad press coverage it received was. The *New York Times* lauded the actions of the Republican idealists and expressed the hope that the party as a whole would share their sentiments. Curtis' *Harper's Weekly* and Godkin's the *Nation* and *New York Evening Post* praised the meeting as well. Throughout the ensuing campaign, frequent and enthusiastic press coverage, thanks to editors and publishers who sympathized with the goals of the reformers, gave the Independents the appearance of a popular and powerful interest group. The Independent Republican activities never slipped by unnoticed during the campaign, and the incessant journalistic barrage turned out to be the reformers' most effective campaign weapon.

It was a period of cutthroat newspaper competition, and journals very often took strong political positions. Political reporting filled the papers, whose editorials minced few words. The Independent Republican journals were no less outspoken than their rivals. As interest in the upcoming conventions quickened, various journals began to comment about the probable candidates. Having acidly disposed of Blaine and Arthur, the Independent papers concluded that Edmunds would be the best Republican candidate. He suffered from a strictly regional appeal, but then, so did the Independent Republicans. A movement centered in New York and New England did not consider a Vermont nominee unthinkable, as many other Americans would. But even the Independents had difficulty generating much enthusiasm about him. An editorial from the March 1, 1884, *Harper's Weekly* noted: "We have no doubt that Mr. Edmunds is at this time the sober preference of the party as an inflexible Republican of spotless personal character, of unquestionable political record, of conceded ability, and of prolonged public experience, who, without trimming or demagoguery, is identified with no faction, and while sure to command the full party vote, would be entirely acceptable to independent voters."

As the Republican national convention in Chicago approached, the Independents struggled to retain their initial momentum and to build or reinforce confidence in Edmunds. Although the reformers had selected Edmunds as a weak but acceptable alternative to the bosses, they went overboard in praising him, an action characteristic of politics in any period. Political campaigning frequently involves image-making and self-delusion, and the Independents practiced both. Curtis, Lodge, Hoar, and countless lesser men convinced themselves that Edmunds would make a fine President. As many Independents came to consider him the only conceivable choice, they redoubled their private efforts to reassure one another and their public efforts to sway the voters. If another acceptable candidate appeared, the Independents might swing away from Edmunds, but the prospect of the party's producing such a man seemed slim as delegates prepared to attend state conventions.

New York State resembled the nation as a whole, with its industrialized urban concentration in the east and its rural areas in the west. The 1880 census had assured it 36 electoral votes, or 9 per cent of the national total of 401. With the solid South lined up on the Democratic side and rock-ribbed Republican states on the other, New York could decide the outcome in 1884. Consequently, political developments in the Empire State attracted especial interest. Adding color to the New York political scene were some of the nation's most famous and infamous machines. While the pre-eminent Tammany Hall in New York City had spawned rivals within its own Democratic party, statewide power had generally fallen to the Republican party. Both factions had suffered in 1882, so that the Stalwarts and the Half-Breeds stood very nearly equal in power in 1884. Roscoe Conkling had retired from the scene in 1881, but many of his erstwhile supporters had maintained their associations and would fall in behind President Arthur. The New York Half-Breeds naturally favored Blaine. Perhaps as a consequence of its having housed two of the most powerful machines in the nation, Democratic Tammany

Hall and Conkling's Stalwarts, New York had also fostered a vigorous Independent Republican group.

The reformers survived their first major partisan skirmish at the Republican State Convention held in Utica in late April of 1884. Republicans in every local jurisdiction had selected delegates to this state conclave. Ordinarily, a state convention routinely reaffirmed local resolutions and selected four delegates-at-large to send to the national convention. Unlike the New York Democratic party, which appointed all of its national delegates at its state convention, the Republicans had divided their authority. The electoral vote is based upon the size of a state's representation in Congress, and the Republicans followed the congressional districting pattern in choosing delegates to their national convention. Local meetings in the state's thirty-four congressional districts had already designated sixty-eight national delegates, two for each electoral vote the state received for its representatives in the House. The state convention had only to select four delegates-at-large, two for each of the senatorial electoral votes. These at-large delegates were usually men with state-wide reputations whom district conventions had overlooked.

In 1884, the selection assumed great significance, because exactly half of the delegates chosen at the district level were already pledged to Blaine. If Blaine supporters could capture the delegate-at-large positions, they could announce that a majority of the state's delegates favored the Plumed Knight, and such an announcement might prove crucial to Blaine's chances at the national convention. The New York backers of President Arthur were particularly concerned, for the incumbent could be considered a native son in his bid for the nomination in his own right, and it would be embarrassing if his home state's delegates voted against him at the national convention.

Almost a quarter of those meeting at Utica identified themselves as reformers. Independent Republicans thus held the balance of power between Blaine's supporters and Arthur's. The latter despaired of obtaining a majority of the national delegation for themselves; they simply did not have enough strength among those already designated. For example, George William Curtis' New York City district had selected the reform editor as its delegate, so the number in Arthur's contingent necessarily fell short of Blaine's. Rather than help the hated Half-Breeds, the President's advocates agreed to side with the Independents and elect four reformers to the at-large positions. The chief of the delegates-at-large, Theodore Roosevelt, had already attracted a great deal of favorable attention in his brief career in the New York Assembly. Thus the reformers from New York sent a vocal young spokesman for their principles and for Edmunds to the national convention. The persistent Stalwart–Half-Breed rivalry forced the delegates to designate neutral Curtis as chairman of the full New York delegation to the national convention in Chicago. The reformers had thus captured the most desirable positions at the New York meeting, although they still remained a small minority of the state's Republican party. Having dealt Blaine's supporters a stinging defeat, the Independents planned to follow it up with more in Chicago.

In analyzing this early skirmish, some contemporary commentators sagely note that, because they represented so small a percentage of the party's total membership, the reformers would have to continue seeking support from others. Common sense would have suggested that the Independents work out deals with one side or the other. Unfortunately, political realities meant less to the reformers than did their principles, so they tended to stand aloof from bargaining sessions. Despite a reluctance to compromise, they had managed to establish themselves in the New York State delegation, and they hoped that continued antagonism between Stalwarts and Blaine supporters would help them in a similar way in Chicago. Consequently, they devoted the two months between the state and national meetings to their own campaign. They aspired to remain an independent force in the Republican party, owing nothing to the regular machines or factions. Increasingly committed to the Edmunds candidacy, the reformers were isolated and correspondingly weak right up to the national convention.

At the opening of the convention on June 3, 1884, Blaine's supporters were obviously the most numerous; a reliable pre-convention estimate placed their number at about 340 of the total 820. Some 280 delegates were pledged to Arthur, a surprisingly large number for the man who had gained the 1880 Vice-Presidential nomination as a sop to Conkling. His impressive show of support indicates the power of the Presidential office. Outside of a major Stalwart remnant in the New York delegation, most of Arthur's delegate strength came from Southern states. The Democratic party dominated state and local politics in the South, and Southern Republican delegates well knew that they could retain their lucrative federal positions only by supporting the incumbent President who had granted them. Thus, the President's patronage alone gave even an unpopular man enormous leverage. A more popular President can almost always be assured of a first-ballot nomination just because of the power his office grants him.

Massachusetts sent the largest contingent of Independents, followed by New York and a few other New England states. The Independent stance did appeal to some politicians from other states, and the reformers hoped that favorite-son supporters would switch to their candidate rather than to either of the front-runners. Before the convention began, however, Edmunds could be sure of only about seventy votes. Bossing one of the best-organized and disciplined machines in the party, Illinois Senator John A. Logan had a delegation that would provide him with almost sixty votes on the first ballot. Although Blaine led the pack, he was well short of the 411 votes necessary for a first-ballot victory. He had come very close in previous conventions and then lost to dark horses, and the Independents hoped for a similar result this time.

The Independent delegates staged a show of strength when an opportunity presented itself almost as soon as the convention opened. As part of its customary opening ceremony, the convention had to select a temporary chairman. The Half-Breed–dominated Republican national committee proposed Powell Clayton, an Arkansas spoilsman. Rumors circulated that Clayton had engineered a deal with the Blaine men, offering to throw his state's delegation to them in return for future patronage. He clearly did not appeal to the reformers, so Henry Cabot Lodge took the floor and proposed as an alternative John R. Lynch, a respected black Representative from Mississippi. Lynch's nomination in opposition to a reputedly corrupt white Southerner clearly revealed the reformers' idealism.

In announcing its choice, the national committee had specifically referred to the Republican party's historic role in guaranteeing the rights of all Southerners. True, General Clayton had fought on the Union side in order to help free the slaves; but the Independent forces went a step further in proposing a black man, whose position on racial issues was unquestionable. Thus the reformers could state that they, too, supported the Republican party's traditional attitudes toward the South. Since both candidates unequivocally represented the Grand Old Party's principles, sectional and racial considerations hardly mattered. The contest, therefore, was concerned almost exclusively with whether or not the convention would accept direction from the pro-Blaine national committee.

Independent spokesmen dominated the ensuing debate. Aside from stressing Clayton's unsuitability, the reformers used the opportunity to announce many of their attitudes toward the party. For example, in his first speech at a national convention, Theodore Roosevelt called upon the delegates to reject dictation from the national committee. This suggestion corresponded with the Independents' criticism that all party organizations gave their leaders too much power. The reformers demanded a roll-call vote to determine who would be temporary chairman, a vote designed to smoke out and identify Blaine men, who were expected to favor Clayton. The roll call dragged on for two hours before Lynch was chosen, winning 424 votes to Clayton's 384. The Blaineites clearly did not control a majority of the delegates at that point, and the Independents congratulated themselves for revealing his weakness at the outset.

As is often the case, conferences and discussions outside the convention would have far more effect on the future than the incidents recorded in the convention's official proceedings. The Independents got a second chance to broadcast their principles, however, when a delegate proposed the following resolution: "Resolved, as the sense of this Convention, that every member of it is bound in honor to support its nominee, whoever that nominee may be; and that no man should hold a seat here who is not ready to so agree." Conkling had championed a similar resolution in 1880, although a technicality had prevented it from coming to a vote. If the resolution passed, the Independents presumably would either have to promise to support Blaine if he were nominated or leave the convention immediately.

Unlike the party's regular members, however, the Independent Republicans considered a party as simply a means to an end. If the means became too warped to achieve the particular end they desired, the reformers reserved the right to drop out. At the 1884 convention, the Independent Republicans had not yet gone this far in their thinking; they still hoped that the party would do the right thing. Early in 1872, the Liberal Republicans had been certain that the Republican party would renominate Grant, so they withdrew before the convention. In 1884, the Independents were not sure what the party would do, and they considered their presence as delegates essential to ensure that the convention made the right decision. Consequently, they righteously disputed the resolution, which would have had an *ex post facto* impact in any case. Arguing against the resolution, George William Curtis resoundingly stated, "A Republican and a free man I came into this Convention. By the grace of God, a Republican and a free man will I go out of this Convention. . . . the presentation of such a resolution in such a Convention as this is a stigma, is an insult to every honorable member who sits here." This and other Independent rhetoric shook the delegates, and the resolution's sponsor withdrew it.

At least one of the convention's essential functions, approving a platform, took place without difficulty on the afternoon of the third day. The chairman of the resolutions committee, Representative William McKinley of Ohio, presented the committee's proposals for the full convention's consideration. The product of lengthy debate and compromise, the suggested planks were relatively few in number and ambiguous in nature. In fact, a single political platform that year would have sufficed for both parties. A universal list of generalizations about tariffs, money, reform, the navy, and so on would have served either party equally well. The Republican policy-makers had included almost every proposal anyone could think of, and they deliberately obscured the party's particular attitude toward the proposals. After a few perfunctory comments, the delegates approved the committee's suggested platform.

A good deal of criticism greeted this platform outside the convention, and many of the Independents inside were equally disappointed, even though some of their spokesmen had helped to frame it. (Curtis had authored the civil service plank, and Lodge the statements concerning the treasury surplus.) It quite accurately spoke for a party that had lost almost all reason for being except to win elections. The same kind of platforms are written even today when no outstanding differences exist between the parties. Predicated upon no great principles, the 1884 Republican platform proposed no startling new policies. Even on the subject of protection, which might have represented one of the few meaningful differences between the parties, the platform proved a model of ambiguity, promising only to correct "inequalities" in the tariffs without abandoning a basic commitment to protection. The platform was so noncontroversial that any man could stand on it. This bothered the Independents as much as anything. Elected upon this bland platform, any Republican who became President would have absolute freedom to do anything he chose. Thus, the personal attitudes and character of the nominee were of vital importance.

The fever of excitement as the Presidential nominating procedure began more than offset the lack of interest exhibited in the platform. Then as now, the states were called in order, and delegates would rise to speak for either a local favorite son or a nationally prominent leader. All the seconding speeches for a particular man came directly after his nomination. Thus the Independents, whose man hailed from Vermont, had to endure a lengthy wait before their chance arrived. Edmunds' advocates were prevented from taking the floor until after midnight. In the absence of a nationally famous Vermonter to perform the task, former Governor John D. Long of Massachusetts did a superb job of proposing the Senator's name to the exhausted delegates, and George William Curtis eloquently seconded the nomination.

The following morning, Presidential balloting began. Blaine received an expected 334½ votes on the first roll call, while Arthur ran second with 278. Edmunds did better than anticipated, polling 93 votes. Logan's machine came through with 83. On the second and third ballots Blaine moved up to 349 and 375, respectively, while Arthur dropped by only a couple of votes. Meanwhile, both Edmunds and Logan lost heavily. As the third ballot drew to a close, Blaine was clearly on the brink of victory. At that moment, the opposing managers might have agreed to a compromise in order to stop the leader. The Arthur delegates were willing to do so, but not the stubbornly idealistic Independents. The essential weakness of a moralistic group in politics is that it cannot compromise its principles even when doomed to defeat. In a desperate bid to gain time, Roosevelt asked for a recess, but the Blaineites would not be denied their victory. The fourth ballot saw the Maine statesman go well over the top with a total of 541 to Arthur's 207 and Edmunds' 41. Logan had chosen this crucial moment to release his delegates to Blaine, and the convention rewarded his efforts with the Vice-Presidential nomination later that evening.

This result, which the Independents considered a disaster, had come about through skillful management. Blaine had attracted a plurality of delegates from the beginning. His managers devoted their attention to making sure that votes wasted on favorite sons during the first ballot would fall to Blaine on subsequent roll calls. Despite the reformers' negative attitude toward him, Blaine represented the first choice of a large portion of his party, and the solid second choice of much of the rest. As the hopelessness of Arthur's candidacy became apparent, many of his partisans acknowledged where the power would lie in the future by switching to Blaine without the slightest qualm. Controlling the strongest remaining Stalwart machine in the nation, Logan withheld support from Blaine, whom he disliked, as long as he could without jeopardizing his own chances of having a say in the upcoming Republican administration. Political self-interest forced him to move when he did. Thus Blaine benefited from the loyal partisanship of the Stalwarts as well as that of his own Half-Breeds. Appearing for the last time as a national faction, the Stalwarts sold out, not to the finicky reformers, who might have rejected their advances in any case, but to the party's new leader. They could at least preserve their machines and their share of the patronage, even if they did not particularly care for the nominee.

The Independents had fallen victim to their own rigidity. Ironically, tieing their aspirations to the fortunes of Edmunds had limited their ability to turn to some other man in the flurry of the balloting. Uncommitted, they could have shifted their support to Senator John Sherman or some other candidate who had a chance of beating Blaine. Instead, they had riveted themselves to a candidacy doomed from the outset, unwilling to cast their votes for Arthur or any other nominee. Perhaps, after all, the Independents really had no business at the national convention. They certainly proved ineffective in fighting the machines and the regular party organizations. Furthermore, when the party rejected their unlikely champion, many of the reformers felt personally rejected as well. Standing amid their shattered hopes, they wondered what to do.

6. The Mugwump Rebellion

. . . the nomination of Messrs. Blaine and Logan by the Republican party [is] a distinct and unqualified repudiation of all its professions of reform, and [is] an insult to the conscience of the country.

—From a resolution approved by the Massachusetts Reform Club, June 7, 1884

The regular partisans had no problems in the wake of the convention. A loyal Republican who had tried and failed to get his favorite chosen would swallow his distaste for the nominee and vote a straight Republican ticket. He need feel no commitment to the candidate himself. The proposed resolution the Independent Republicans had shouted down at the convention outlined the usual pattern. Those who participated in a party's deliberations ordinarily felt a responsibility to support whomever the party nominated. Blaine had won the nomination without obvious irregularities; regular party members would vote for him. In order to survive, the organization demanded loyalty, above any consideration of the merits of the individual put forward.

The Independent Republicans hardly qualified as regular partisans. They belonged to no machine; they did not expect rewards from the spoils system; they did not even represent a well-organized faction within the party. Above all, they did not consider party loyalty the primary ideal to which a man should aspire. The dictates of their consciences mattered more to them than all the persuasions and seductions the party organization might offer. Throughout the spring, they had succeeded in convincing themselves that the nomination and election of James G. Blaine would be an unmitigated catastrophe. In the absence of a more compelling reason to support the Republican party, they had allowed the issue of public honesty to assume supremacy in their own minds. Convinced that Blaine's election would undermine that principle, they could not assist him. Many therefore decided it was impossible for them to continue associating with a party which, in their eyes, had just proved itself unrepentant.

Consequently, individually or in groups, many reformers deserted their party, as they had been threatening to do for months. It was no longer their party in any case, but seemed to belong to the bosses and to Blaine. The rebels justified their actions on moral principles which they claimed the party had long ago subordinated to expediency. The *New York Times*, supporting their actions, disgustedly declared that the Blaine-Logan ticket stood "for everything the Republican party must get rid of in order to be of any use to the country." The yoking together of the popular Half-Breed leader with an equally notorious Stalwart boss was simply too much.

The rebel group included many men who had been Liberal Republicans in 1872 as well as others who had exhibited independent thinking in other ways during earlier political confrontations. But the Independent Republican appellation was loosely defined and applied to men with various levels of commitment to reform. Some had hidden behind the name in confusion while deciding what role they should play in the party. Others sincerely used it as a challenge to the party bosses, threatening to revolt if ignored. Therefore, not every previously proclaimed Independent Republican felt the need to leave the party. Many of these men rejected true independence and remained steadfast to the regular party.

The Blaine nomination thus served to sift out the resolute reformers from the mere hangers-on. Social pressure worked both ways. Stanch party members bitterly criticized the rebels, while the Independents who had already revolted encouraged the hesitant to leave as well. Caught in an emotional cross fire of reform sentiments and old loyalties, many an Independent had to undergo much soul-searching in order to decide which way to turn. The stronger and older his party ties, the more difficult he found the ultimate separation.

George William Curtis exhibited all the characteristics of a man torn between his reform principles and his lifelong partisan commitments. Having served the party for over a quarter of a century, he considered himself a thorough Republican. He had recently participated prominently in the New York State Convention, which had chosen him to head his state's delegation to Chicago. His involvement in the party was correspondingly very strong indeed. In the end, his commitment to ideals turned out to be stronger. Curtis stayed on through the closing ceremonies of the convention, feeling a primary obligation to those who had sent him as their representative. But once he returned to New York, he became the free man he had dramatically proclaimed himself to be and left the party.

Curtis actually had little freedom of choice; his decision had already been made for him. He had just written a series of editorials for *Harper's Weekly* attacking Blaine. Thomas Nast, his most renowned staff member, had depicted Blaine in his cartoons as posing a major threat to the party, and Nast himself hesitated scarcely at all in repudiating the party. The Harper family, who published the magazine, had provided funds and offered services to the early anti-Blaine organization. With all of his close associates in the reform movement renouncing their party affiliations, Curtis could hardly have remained isolated. By mid-July, he had assumed his preordained position at the head of the rebellion.

The other leading light of the developing revolt, Carl Schurz, suffered no such period of indecision. He had attended the convention, not as a delegate, but simply as an observer. When Blaine won the requisite number of votes for his nomination, Schurz reportedly announced to those sitting nearby, "That is the hour and the minute which will go down in history as marking the death of the Republican party." His suspicion of Blaine left him no alternative but to bolt. He probably felt more comfortable than Curtis as a rebel, since Schurz had been a Liberal dissenter from the regular party in 1872. His previous refusal to associate with what he considered a morally corrupt party permitted Schurz to make his decision to do so again with great resolution. He would become the bolters' most prominent and energetic speaker in the upcoming campaign.

Members of Republican and reform clubs in New York and Massachusetts rebelled en masse. Particularly in Boston, the revolt became socially acceptable in upper-class circles. Those who did not make the move were viewed with suspicion and sometimes were even socially ostracized. Both old and young alike broke with the party. Although they formally retained the Independent Republican title, indicating their continuing attachment to the old party's ideals, they earned a number of more widely used nicknames. The favorite was Mugwump, a term that had been used in 1872 to characterize the Liberal Republicans as well and that derived from an Algonquin Indian word referring to a young chieftain. Critics of the Independents redefined it to mean a callow youth who claimed to know more than his elders. A facetious definition of the times claimed that a Mugwump was an indecisive bird who sat on the fence with his mug on one side and his wump on the other. This description fit the 1884 revolters perfectly, for they had stopped participating in one of the regular parties without deciding what to do with themselves next. The bolters themselves eventually developed a sentimental attachment to the term Mugwump, defining it as a man of principle willing to stand up for his convictions. Although the rebels continued to call themselves Independent Republicans throughout the campaign of 1884, the Mugwump appellation became the popular method of designating dissenters from the regular Republican party.

As individual journalists left the party, their papers also shifted allegiance. *Harper's Weekly* became the leading Mugwump organ even as Curtis made his decision. E. L. Godkin remained attracted to the Republican party's traditions and earlier principles but found that he, too, had to part company with the organization when it nominated Blaine. Both his weekly *Nation* and his daily *New York Evening Post* became Mugwump journals. Already an illustrious member of the nation's press, the *New York Times* followed the predilections of its owner and publisher, George Jones, out of the Republican fold and into the Mugwump no man's land. The most surprising change involved James Gordon Bennett, son and namesake of the founder of the *New York Herald*. Bennett had always been an ultrapartisan Republican editor, but he could not stomach Blaine. Never an Independent Republican journal, the *Herald* had devoted its preconvention activities to a defense of incumbent President Arthur. When Arthur's hopes fell before the Blaine onslaught, the *Herald* leaped onto the Mugwump bandwagon. In Boston, both the *Herald* and the *Transcript* bolted the Republican party and began to inundate that city with Mugwump propaganda. In Springfield, Massachusetts, the *Republican* denied the verity of its name by quitting the regular party.

The Mugwump walkout embarrassed loyal Republicans almost as much as it angered them. They had not been able to believe that the Independents would actually take such a step. Once Blaine won the nomination, the regulars thought, the reformers' protests would subside and, if they would not actively campaign for the ticket, at least they would vote for it. The flaw in this assumption stemmed from the Blaineites' mistaking the sincerity of Independent threats and assertions for typical partisan rhetoric.

The most acid criticisms of the revolt appeared in Whitelaw Reid's *New York Tribune*, a journal that had stood staunchly behind Blaine from the beginning. Reid's contempt for anyone who left the party made strange reading in the paper Liberal Republican candidate Horace Greeley had founded. The *Tribune* embroidered on the theme that those who had claimed to be Republicans before the nomination had undertaken a solemn obligation to support the party's regularly chosen candidate. The Mugwumps rejected this deterministic logic. Instead, they felt that they were pursuing a proper course while the Republican partisans were failing in their larger duty to the nation. As *Harper's Weekly* pointed out, to say "that the party must be sustained at all costs is to say that, whatever it does, the party ought to be supported. A more slavish doctrine, and one more utterly unworthy of intelligent American citizens, cannot be imagined. It is because the men who formed the Republican party spurned such a doctrine that slavery has been abolished, and the republic saved." Here the Mugwump journal struck a vulnerable spot. The idealistic men who had breathed life into the early Republican party had boldly favored throwing over the old, decadent, political organizations and standing up for a new set of principles. Thus, the Independents concluded, Mugwumps were as deserving of commendation in revolting from a corrupt party as the Grand Old Party's charter members had been.

So sincerely did the Independents believe they were right and the remaining Republicans wrong that they went a step further, claiming that only their drastic action could ultimately destroy the evil that had swept over the party. They insisted that they were still Republicans, loyal not to the party's present leaders but to its great traditions. The Mugwumps cared nothing for the petty patronage that might filter to them if they stayed in the party. They had concluded that the government their own party provided was corrupt and must be overthrown. Civil-service reform would assist in this task, but the shock of their bolt and the consequent self-analysis it would stimulate in the party might do much more. As the *New York Times* editorialized, the defeat of Blaine "will be the salvation of the Republican party. It will arouse its torpid conscience, it will stir it to self-purification, it will depose the false leaders who have fastened themselves upon it, it will send the rogues to the background, and will make the party once more worthy of power in the Republic it has so nobly served."

Mugwumpery became the subject of lively political discussion throughout the nation. Day after day, the party press devoted editorials and criticism to the revolt. But that this controversy seriously influenced the attitudes of the party's machine leaders remains doubtful. The regular Republicans considered party disloyalty a sin. As they ordered their values, party loyalty came first and conscience second. In attempting to understand the Mugwumps, regular Republicans ascribed the revolt to causes other than the idealistic ones the bolters proclaimed. For example, according to a popular Republican contention, the Mugwumps had revoted because they disagreed with the party's high tariff policies. The *Times* and particularly the *Post,* under Godkin's British influence, had called for a reduction of tariff rates during the preceding spring. But a good many reformers favored continued protection, so this explanation proved unsatisfactory. The regular Republicans could never admit that the reform ideals were sufficient to precipitate the Mugwump revolt, and they continued to try to find other explanations for the phenomenon.

The Independents parried every criticism. The rejoinders the Mugwumps hurled back at the party seem unduly self-righteous in retrospect as the Independent Republicans had stayed with the party until well into the campaign year. This fact alone, however, may have embittered the rebels. They had participated in the party for years, hopeful that it would eventually realize that its true interests coincided with theirs. They had observed the internecine factional struggles with increasing dismay, but as long as that combat continued, the capacity for evil of either faction remained limited. At their February meeting in 1884, the Independents had essentially given the party notice that it must adopt their principles or they would leave. The vituperative postconvention Mugwump rhetoric represented the welling over of years of dammed-up feelings of disgust and disappointment.

Despite such circumstances, many Independents chose not to reject the Blaine nomination. The division that developed in the reformers' ranks made the rebellion seem inexplicable to some outsiders, yet the differences between the Mugwumps and the Independents who stayed behind can be stated simply: those who stuck with the party felt that they could do more for themselves and the party from within. The Mugwumps hoped that their revolt would bring about a rededication to principles in the Republican party. But it might also skim all the principled men off the top, leaving an unrepentant organization behind.

Theodore Roosevelt ultimately benefited most from continued adherence to the Republican party. Other young men possessing similar backgrounds and reform attitudes were prominent in the bolt from the party. Roosevelt, however, had already served his party in an important capacity in the New York Assembly and, like Curtis, felt he owed the party abstraction at least some consideration for giving him a position of trust. Furthermore, the 1884 New York State Convention had chosen Roosevelt to lead its delegates-at-large in Chicago. As an upper-class, urban-bred Republican, he naturally fell in with those interested in bettering their party. He had previously spoken for reform, and he refused to support the Blaine candidacy as long as an alternative seemed to exist within the party. At the national convention, Roosevelt had done as much and, given his volatile personality, probably even more than many of the Independents in trying to capture the nomination for someone other than Blaine. When the Plumed Knight won, Roosevelt was undecided about what to do next.

Roosevelt had ample reason to brood in 1884. Both his wife and his mother had recently died, leaving him emotionally drained. Roosevelt spent the summer months on his Dakota ranch, away from the incessant pressures of the New York Mugwumps. His good friend Henry Cabot Lodge, another vacillating Independent Republican, corresponded with him and served as one of his few contacts with the political world. Eventually Roosevelt decided to remain loyal to the party. He rationalized his decision by arguing that a loyal Republican should support his party's regularly selected nominees. If Blaine turned out to be a terrible President, Roosevelt concluded, it would be no more than the party deserved. Thus the young partisan begged the question of his own responsibility, permitting the party label and party loyalty to decide for him. By October, Roosevelt had returned to the East, where he campaigned for regular Republican candidates and publicly denounced the Mugwumps as traitors. Steadfast Republican Theodore Roosevelt would not consider bolting his party simply because its convention had chosen the wrong nominee, at least not until 1912, when the party spurned his own Presidential candidacy as a Progressive Republican.

Rumors circulated that Henry Cabot Lodge had coerced young Roosevelt, although Lodge later insisted that no one could exert such persuasive power over the willful New Yorker. The two men had apparently agreed before the convention that, if Blaine was selected, they would have to go along with the choice.

Immediately after the nomination, however, Lodge encountered strong pressures to revolt as hundreds of his friends and compatriots severed their party bonds. But Lodge had even more to lose than Roosevelt, for he had deliberately chosen to pursue politics as a career. A professional politician needed a party. An Independent candidate might win a race now and then, but for security and guaranteed advancement, party backing remained essential. Consequently, Lodge had little choice but to stay with his party. Personal ambition played a deciding role in his commitment to the party that offered him a chance to attain the goals he had set for himself. A precipitous withdrawal would have destroyed his promising political career in a moment.

Lodge suffered dearly for his loyalty. The members of his social set in Boston had almost wholly gone over to Mugwumpery. His long-standing friendships with Carl Schurz and Moorfield Storey collapsed abruptly. He nearly lost his seat on the Harvard Board of Overseers, and he had to resign from the Massachusetts Reform Club, which had become the nation's leading Mugwump organization. There were compensations as well, for his loyalty in a time of trial impressed party leaders. As chairman of the Massachusetts State Republican Committee, he had more than enough work to occupy his time. In September he accepted the Republican nomination for a seat in the United States House of Representatives. Although he lost his bid for election in 1884, no doubt because of Mugwump defections, he won a House seat two years later. The Massachusetts legislature elevated him to the Senate in 1893, where he served until his death in 1924, having become the most influential senator in the United States.

A current senator from Massachusetts, George F. Hoar, was another Independent who did not rebel. Hoar and Roosevelt stood at opposite ends of the political ladder. The older man had no higher ambition than to complete his career of public service in the Senate. At the national convention he had chaired the Massachusetts delegation, which contained a larger percentage of Independents than any other delegation at the meeting. Hoar agreed with every Independent and Mugwump idea except one: that a man might in good conscience repudiate his party. A crusading reformer, Hoar felt that improvement of the party system could be accomplished only by working within that system. Fortunately for him, he did not share the usual Mugwump distrust of Blaine, even though he would have been happier with another candidate, especially his good friend Edmunds. Hoar denounced the Mugwumps throughout the campaign and he continued to deride party bolters as contemptuous until he himself broke with the party in 1899, when it favored annexing the Philippine Islands. Eventually, then, both Hoar and Roosevelt reacted as true Independents, although neither considered Blaine's nomination reason enough to sever their party connections.

These three men exemplify the Independents who stayed with the party. As a young man just beginning his political career, Roosevelt felt that party membership offered him a future. The revolt caught Lodge in the midst of an already established career, and he knew he would lose much by bolting. Hoar, already at the pinnacle of his profession, did not need to revolt to gain attention and consideration for his reform ideas. Significantly, only Carl Schurz among the leading professional Republican politicians did rebel, and he was not holding a political job at the time. As a strictly personal emotion, party loyalty assumed more or less importance depending upon what one expected in return. The party had achieved sufficient stability by 1884 to ensure offices and prominence to its adherents. In addition, the Republican party still carried an aura of respectability that helped even the most sincere reformer to justify his loyalty. Fundamental to all other considerations was the indisputable fact that Blaine had been the popular choice at the convention. If the party's will meant anything, Blaine had deserved his nomination.

Those who stayed with the party at least knew exactly how to behave in the upcoming months. Party formulas guided all their political decisions and actions. The bolters, however, had jumped from the security of party into a limbo outside. Political activists lacking a party, they represented an anomaly in American politics. The two-party tradition had already become so well established that those who were not members of one major party were assumed to support the other. The splinter groups which built tenuous structures intended either to become a major party or to force one of the major parties to adopt their principles. The Mugwumps possessed no such clear plan of action after the convention. They had rebelled strictly in reaction to the Blaine nomination. How they should proceed remained uncertain to the Mugwumps themselves.

An obvious first step would be to establish some kind of organization. An unorganized protest group could hardly affect the outcome. Hundreds or even thousands of men deciding privately to snub a particular candidate would, of course, have some effect on the election. These same men organized and actively propagandizing would have a substantial influence on the campaign as well and would probably convince others to vote their way in the election. The rebelling Independents wanted to punish the Republican party for nominating a man they considered corrupt. An organized protest group would be most effective in achieving this goal. In addition, an organization would give the rebels a sense of security and unity that would prevent some from backsliding. They needed one another's reassurance to maintain their convictions as they faced the prospect of fighting a highly organized political party. Finally, political activists accustomed to participating in organizations would feel uncomfortable without one. Committees, clubs, and discussion groups had always played an important part in the American way of life. The Mugwumps could hardly avoid following a pattern ingrained in the national character.

Certain existing groups helped the rebels to find themselves immediately. In the early days of the Mugwump revolt, the Massachusetts Reform Club in Boston assumed leadership. On June 7, the day after the fateful decision in Chicago, members of the club passed several resolutions and formed a committee to correspond with other anti-Blaine Republicans and coordinate national activities. The first resolution openly stated the feelings of Mugwumps throughout the country: "Voted, that the Massachusetts Reform Club regards the nomination of Messrs. Blaine and Logan by the Republican party as a distinct and unqualified repudiation of all its professions of reform, and as an insult to the conscience of the country, and that the members of the club will under no circumstances support them." The club's prompt action suggests that its members had already thoroughly discussed how they would react if Blaine were nominated.

The coordinating committee met during the following week in the office of Josiah Quincy, a writer and historian whose famous family included three of Boston's mayors. To dramatize their resolve and encourage converts, the committee decided to stage a public meeting on Friday, June 13. More than 1400 Independents signed the call for the meeting, which appeared in Boston newspapers. The meeting itself proved quite successful, with Thomas Wentworth Higginson, President Charles Eliot of Harvard College, and others delivering addresses to the assemblage. The group selected a Committee of One Hundred to coordinate Mugwump activities in the Bay State. Twenty-five of the members made plans to attend the National Independent Republican Conference to meet in New York City the following week.

The New Yorkers were slower to move, for they lacked an existing organization to spearhead their activities. In fact, the first major Mugwump gathering in the Empire State was the one the Massachusetts committee sent its members to attend. A private rather than a public meeting, the conclave took place at the home of publisher J. Henry Harper on June 17. The location was symbolic, for the Mugwump press assisted immeasurably in the months to come. All the familiar New York Independents who had rebelled attended the meeting, which approved and reiterated the Massachusetts resolution. In addition, the Mugwumps set up a national committee to coordinate activities and serve as a central clearing house for their ideas and speakers.

At both the Massachusetts and New York meetings, discussion of tactics the Mugwumps should employ assumed high priority. Among the possibilities was the formation of a protest party similar to the Liberal Republican effort in 1872. Few found this proposal acceptable, however, in view of the disappointing outcome of the earlier campaign. Like the 1872 Liberals, the 1884 Mugwumps were hindered by the lack of an outstanding candidate of their own. This circumstance had weakened the Independents at the Republican convention, where they had settled upon unexciting Edmunds to run against Blaine. Edmunds had not bolted, nor would he, although his tepid support did little to help Blaine. In any case, he would hardly have attracted much support away from the regular Republican ticket. The rebelling Independents could probably have put together a ticket if they had to, but it would have been doomed from the start and would most likely have helped the Democrats to defeat Blaine.

In fact, a Democratic victory seemed to be the most likely result of almost anything the Mugwumps did, and they had already considered what this eventuality meant. The readiness of the Independents to bolt in 1884 depended in large measure upon the Democratic party's growing respectability. The Independents felt that the Republican party had sunk so deeply into partisan corruption that its opposition did not appear worse in comparison. Had no safe Democratic alternative existed, notably in the person of New York Governor Grover Cleveland, the Mugwumps would very probably never have revolted. The two-party system was supposed to give the voters a choice, but until recently the Democratic party had not represented an acceptable alternative for Republican reformers. Now they felt the equation had changed significantly.

Consequently, both the Massachusetts Reform Club and the New York meeting decided upon a wait-and-see policy. They had absolutely ruled out supporting the regular Republican ticket, but they intended to remain uncommitted until the Democratic National Convention had chosen its candidates. If the Democratic nominee was acceptable to the idealistic Independents, they were not unwilling to devote their full energies to helping elect him. After the Democratic convention, the Republican rebels planned to gather again to decide whether to support the Democratic ticket or nominate a more or less hopeless one of their own. All Mugwump and indeed most national attention thus became focused upon the Democratic party. Whatever their national convention did, the Democrats would pay much more attention to their own desires and obligations than to those of some dissident Independent Republicans. Thus, the recent history of the Democratic party and its contenders for the Presidential nomination assumed crucial importance for the Mugwumps.

7. The Democratic Organization

If the Democrats fritter away their chances this time, when everything conspires to present them the finest opportunities, there will be no resurrection for them.

> —CARL SCHURZ, in a letter to Thomas F. Bayard, July 2, 1884

The Democratic party after the Civil War resembled the prewar one in catering to local issues. The early coalition had been able to survive because its leaders exerted little unifying pressure. Therefore, the federal policies the national Democratic party had promoted generally interfered but little with local interests. States' rights had represented a fundamental Democratic tenet. The party's ability to endure up to and even through the sectional breakdown of the 1850's and 1860's depended to a large degree upon the freedom local leaders enjoyed. Former Confederate military officers and civil servants proliferated in the party that rose to oust Reconstruction Republicans from offices in the South. The border states had produced a sizable number of Union Democrats, loyal to the federal government but unimpressed with the Eastern-bred leadership of the Republican party. Although only at a token level in some cases, a Democratic opposition party had continued to operate throughout the North.

The local orientation of the various elements of the Democratic party was apparent in its urban machines. Proclaiming friendship for workingmen and immigrants, these machines infiltrated and solidified their power in the brawling cities of an increasingly industrial and urban nation. The machines maintained themselves and grew stronger through local politicking and regional victories, extorting abundant rewards from the national party whenever it managed to score a success. Meanwhile Republican excesses helped to improve the Democrats' national reputation. Given the opportunity, they might well prove as corrupt as the worst Republican spoilsmen, but since they lacked the chance, they escaped the label. Democratic reformers concentrated their attention on local machines, as Tilden had done in fighting Tammany Hall, rather than on national abuses. At the national level, the Democrats did not need to discriminate between good and bad Republicans; they simply dismissed all members of the Grand Old Party as unworthy of support.

Eventually the Democrats created an image of solid respectability through the development of the Bourbon Democracy, a loose aggregation of Southern and Northern conservatives. The Bourbons, who represented the party's businessmen, intended to prevent the party organization from falling into the hands of the farmers and laborers among its constituency. Perhaps the most important determinant of a businessman's political affiliation was his conception of the proper role of government. The Republicans favored an active role, at least to the extent of having the government protect manufacturers and encourage industrialization. Bourbon Democrats wanted to limit the government's activities to the bare minimum, much as Jefferson and Jackson had. A low-tariff advocate almost invariably supported the Bourbon philosophy. Influential and wealthy businessmen, particularly railroad owners and traders who derived much of their income from foreign commerce, became Bourbons and gave the Democratic party the financial support so essential to its political success. The Bourbons had supported Tilden for the New York governorship in 1874 and for the Presidency two years later. Although they lost in 1876, the Democrats had established themselves as a serious opposition party to the Republicans. Therefore they were ready to act in 1882, when an economic recession set in.

Throughout the nation, local issues clouded the national political picture. The Democratic party gained control of the House of Representatives but simultaneously lost Senate seats, giving the Republicans the edge there. The Democratic showing in state and local elections was impressive. New York, Ohio, Pennsylvania, and Massachusetts elected Democratic governors. The most serious Republican blunders had occurred in the most critical state in the Union, New York. For several years the struggle among Stalwarts, Half-Breeds, and Independents had threatened to split apart the Republican party in the Empire State. In the 1882 gubernatorial race, the uneasy Republican coalition broke down at last, opening the way for the elevation of Grover Cleveland, the man who would ultimately bring about the Republican downfall at the national level as well.

The chaotic New York political scene in 1882 involved many familiar faces. In the four years since President Hayes had thrown the two Stalwarts out of the New York Customhouse, Chester Arthur had managed to move into the White House and Alonzo Cornell into the governor's mansion in Albany. But as their paths had diverged, so had their outlooks. Governor Cornell had carefully cultivated his own loyal band of supporters, so he was no longer dependent upon Roscoe Conkling by the time the Senator retired. As governor, Cornell had done a fairly decent job of running the state government, and even the Half-Breeds were impressed with his administrative abilities. The Independents refused to ignore his machine background, and no one who had been a Scratcher in 1879 would ever vote for him. Nevertheless, with a little luck, incumbent Cornell might easily overcome that drawback in attaining the re-election he dearly wanted. Cornell exhibited no interest in helping Arthur, probably correctly assuming that the President had no chance of winning the nomination in any case and could give him no help.

Meanwhile, like everyone else, President Arthur was thinking ahead to the 1884 Presidential race, in which he, too, desired re-election. He had little sure support besides the federal officers in the South, particularly now that many Stalwarts stood behind Cornell in the President's home state. Consequently, Arthur determined to replace Governor Cornell with a man both more loyal to him and more amenable to suggestion, in order to create strong backing for himself in New York. He chose Secretary of the Treasury Charles Folger as his stalking horse and, through some heavy-handed patronage manipulation, got the state Republican convention to nominate his man. Happy to see Cornell lose but disgusted by the process, many Independents decided once again to scratch the Republican ticket. Half-Breeds who hoped to dominate the Presidential sweepstakes in 1884 with their choice, Blaine, were also annoyed by the President's actions. Finally, many of Cornell's outflanked Stalwart supporters wanted to avenge their chief. Thus, members of all three major segments of the Republican party were displeased with the nominee, and many thought of following the 1879 Scratchers' precedent on election day. Ironically, this Republican factionalism ruined the career of Charles Folger, one of the better administrators in the Republican party.

At their state convention, the Democrats mulled over several possible opponents for Folger and eventually settled upon a man who had just begun to make headlines as mayor of Buffalo. Although Grover Cleveland's name could hardly be considered a household word, his obscurity meant that he had not yet alienated many members of his party. In a moment of virtually unprecedented party unity, all the Democrats, from the conservative, moneyed Bourbons to the self-seeking Tammany Braves, agreed upon Cleveland. They continued to work together throughout the campaign and turned out en masse on election day. Cleveland appeared to be so uncontroversial that many Scratchers felt they could vote for him without jeopardizing their principles. Furthermore, disappointed regular Republicans who wanted to make certain that Arthur's plans went awry did more than refuse to vote for Folger—they cast Cleveland ballots.

Although the national tide generally ran in the Democrats' favor in 1882, Cleveland's stupendous victory outshone all other successes. He swept into office with a majority of more than 192,000 votes out of about 900,000 cast. The Democrats, conveniently overlooking the source of many of his votes, proclaimed a great partisan victory. Overnight, the obscure Cleveland became a national figure. Any governor of New York automatically became a Presidential prospect, and the fantastic majority Cleveland had run up made his selection almost certain.

Despite all the speculation, the American people knew almost nothing about Cleveland, but his unremarkable story soon became public knowledge. Stephen Grover Cleveland was born in New Jersey in 1837, one of several children of a Presbyterian minister who died while Grover was still a boy. As the young man had to work to help his family make ends meet, his schooling was frequently interrupted. Eventually he read law, was admitted to the bar, and entered practice. Meanwhile he remained unmarried in order to help support his mother's family while his two brothers went off to fight in the Civil War. When drafted, Cleveland sent a substitute, hired for $150. Later he served as sheriff of Erie County for a couple of terms, but then he dropped out of public life to devote his attention to his private law practice, which had become fairly profitable.

Cleveland maintained more than an amateur's interest in politics, however. He knew many Democratic leaders in Buffalo and had always voted Democratic. In 1881, when he was still a relatively young man of 44, local party leaders convinced him to accept the Democratic nomination for mayor of Buffalo. Apparently hesitant about taking the job, he expressed his reluctance to move upward at each step on the political ladder during the next few years. Success bred ambition, however, and, given the opportunity, he served to the best of his ability. Above all, he cultivated an image of absolute honesty in his political behavior. As mayor of Buffalo, he earned a reputation as a reformer by cleaning up much of the corruption that had characterized the city's government. His reform reputation helped at the state convention in 1882 when reform had become a leading national issue. At the same time, he was not so active a reformer as to disturb the machine elements in the party, which were more interested in nominating a winning candidate than in his principles. As it turned out, with the New York Republican party so hopelessly shattered, the Democrats probably could have nominated and elected almost anyone that year.

As governor, Cleveland was increasingly irritated by State Senator Thomas Grady, a leading Tammany representative, and he finally asked Tammany boss John Kelly not to return Grady to Albany, a request which Kelly ignored. The antagonism between Tammany Hall and Cleveland worsened in the succeeding months and threatened to undermine critically his Democratic support in the state. Otherwise, Cleveland performed well as far as his party was concerned. He relied primarily upon the state's conservative leadership, which had become powerful a few years earlier. Never a machine man, Cleveland discovered that party manager Daniel Manning offered him wise advice as well as support from the Bourbon elements when he needed it. Further, Cleveland's own conservative political views corresponded with those of the Bourbons. Therefore he generally cooperated with them, although he remained stubbornly independent on some matters.

During his short term in the governor's office, Cleveland did little to alter his image as a noncontroversial politician. He did not introduce any radical programs, nor did he dynamically carry any out. He saw the role of governor, as he would that of President, as a sort of quality controller for measures approved by the legislative branch. If he considered a bill detrimental to the public welfare, he did not hesitate to use his veto power. He handled every chore in the same methodical way he had conducted his law practice, never completely trusting anyone else's suggestions or advice until he had checked things out himself. Under Cleveland, the process of governing was slow and careful, with few chances taken or opportunities seized.

His reputation made Cleveland appealing to the reformers. His attitude toward the New York civil-service-reform program that Roosevelt had guided through the state legislature compared favorably with that of President Arthur at the national level. Cleveland had approved the program and had chosen distinguished men to administer it, including the leading reformer, Silas W. Burt. Cleveland made no effort to placate all his critics.

Indeed, Roosevelt complained bitterly about the Governor's veto of certain reform bills on the grounds that they were improperly drafted. Roosevelt claimed that Cleveland was merely trying to protect some Bourbon officeholders from removal. In the eyes of most other Independent Republicans, Cleveland's basic advantage over his fellow politicians lay in his relative newness to the game and his consequent lack of connections to machines. Manning and other managers scrupulously remained in the background except during campaigns, and Cleveland would not have responded favorably if they had interfered with his administration. His dispute with Grady earned the full sympathy of many an Independent. Cleveland had not yet become a corrupt partisan, and the reformers hoped that he would retain his indifference to machine enticements.

On the other hand, his lack of experience might also be considered something of a drawback. The reformers had a few qualms about the Governor's administrative capabilities. In his comparatively short political career, he had had too little time to become a seasoned administrator. So far he had done an adequate if unspectacular job; presumably he could continue to do so.

As the National Democratic Convention approached, a good deal of attention focused upon Cleveland's relationship with Samuel J. Tilden, the 1876 Democratic Presidential candidate and former governor of New York. Tilden's name cropped up frequently in discussions of Democratic Presidential plans, although his intimate associates recognized that he had become too ill even to campaign, much less to handle the Presidency if he won. He had turned down the 1880 nomination for reasons of health, and his health had further deteriorated by 1884. Although he remained titular head of the party, his influence on current activities and certainly his future capabilities were negligible. For his part, Cleveland pretty much ignored Tilden, and Daniel Manning saw to it that neither man felt threatened by the other. A close confidant of Tilden's for years, Manning knew that the old man could not run. Nevertheless, the wily manager did not interfere with the periodic Tilden booms, for they kept other candidates' names from looming too large and would do no harm when Manning eventually put Cleveland forward.

The New York Governor's only serious rival for the nomination was Senator Thomas F. Bayard of Delaware. Bayard, an undistinguished man in many respects, currently headed the family that had run Delaware as a sort of political fiefdom since the beginning of the century. His availability stemmed largely from the absence of other Democratic contenders for the Presidential nomination. He had been considered at previous national conventions, but his small state would make almost no difference in the electoral vote count. Also, being from a border state, Bayard had made some statements during the sectional crisis that still rankled in the North. The great popularity he enjoyed in the South would prove redundant since the Southern states would give their electoral support to virtually anyone the Democratic party nominated.

Consequently, the most important problem facing Cleveland's advocates was how to get his name before the national convention most effectively. In this endeavor, the Mugwumps proved quite helpful. The probability that Cleveland would capture the Democratic nomination had served as one of the mainsprings motivating the Independent revolt. During the spring of 1884, as it had criticized the possible candidates of its own party, with particular emphasis on Blaine, the Independent press had been kind to the Governor. The Independent Republicans from New York, who served as the movement's leading propagandists, had observed him in action at close quarters, and Cleveland had not disappointed them. When they bailed out of their own party, Cleveland was their parachute.

As the date for the Democratic national convention approached, the Mugwumps showered Cleveland with praise. Having decided to await the Democratic party's decision, they hoped and expected it would be for Cleveland. They observed the party's actions with some trepidation, for that erratic group had previously distinguished itself by making some very illogical decisions. The reform press tried to convince the Democrats that the Governor offered their best chance of success. How closely the Democrats heeded Mugwump advice is doubtful, but the reformers continued to give that advice freely in any case. The Independents realized that some of his own partisans had become unhappy with Cleveland's actions, but they did not consider this a drawback. As *Harper's* commented, "Such feeling of opposition to him as exists in his party is most flattering and significant, because it springs from dislike of the official uprightness, courage, and independence which he has displayed. These are the very qualities which, in the absence of overpowering national issues, and when the chief public interest is that of administration, are most desirable in the Executive." Here, of course, the journal stated a favorite Mugwump assumption: that everyone was vitally interested in reform of the administrative branch of the government. Whether or not this assumption was correct, the widely held belief that Cleveland had alienated only the unworthy and corrupt helped his chances. According to Mugwump critics, such men abounded at Tammany Hall, and the fewer dealings Cleveland had with them the better. The Tammany Braves obviously had little interest in furthering the career of the Governor they had come to dislike thoroughly, except possibly to make him President and get him out of Albany.

Taking charge of Cleveland's 1884 effort, Daniel Manning considered the New York state convention crucial. It was held at Syracuse on June 18, more than a week after the national Republican convention had nominated Blaine. Just before it convened, Tilden issued a disclaimer of any intention to run, thus freeing Manning to boost Cleveland. The key question at the New York convention concerned what attitude Tammany Hall would take. If the machine discouraged its supporters from voting for Cleveland, he would probably lose to Blaine, as the Mugwump contingent likely to support him would not be large enough to offset a full scale Tammany rebellion. If, on the other hand, Tammany leaders decided to support the party's regularly nominated candidate, the Democrats stood a good chance of winning the state's electoral votes, which would be essential for a Democratic victory. If a Democrat became President with its help, Tammany Hall would earn control of a sizable share of the federal patronage. The machine had proved itself capable of survival and growth without federal spoils, but astute political bosses knew well the advantages federal offices could bring to a machine.

Obviously, Manning faced a ticklish task in trying to unite the state party behind Cleveland.

The state convention had to select the full complement of seventy-two delegates to the national conclave. This differed markedly from the Republican procedure, in which district conventions selected delegates to represent their districts at the national convention, and the state convention had only to designate four delegates-at-large. New York City's three major Democratic organizations, Tammany Hall, Irving Hall, and the County Democracy, each hoped to control a majority of the national convention delegates sent from the city. In a compromise finally hammered out at Saratoga, Tammany and the County Democracy obtained an equal number of national-delegate seats, while the weaker Irving Hall received a much smaller share. Fortunately for the Governor's chances, the convention named Daniel Manning as chairman of the full delegation, enabling this talented manager to superintend Cleveland's affairs from an influential position.

Cognizant of a need for caution, Manning did not insist that the state convention endorse a particular nominee prior to the delegates' departure for the national convention. He probably could have obtained an endorsement for Cleveland, but not without making public the strong opposition Tammany felt toward him. By keeping this opposition as quiet as possible, Manning may have helped to prevent an early categorical rejection of Cleveland by Tammany leaders. Besides, Manning could take advantage of an alternative method of making sure the delegation would support Cleveland. Under his guidance, the state convention instructed its delegation to use the unit rule, a device that forced it to cast all seventy-two of its votes for whichever candidate received a majority of the delegates' support. The Republicans had outlawed the use of the unit rule in an overdue attempt at party reform, but the option still remained available to Democrats. Once the delegates reached the national convention, all Manning had to do was make sure that a majority of them supported Cleveland. Therefore, the New Yorkers headed for Chicago uninstructed, but wearing the unit-rule strait jacket.

The Democrats had chosen to hold their convention in the

same building in the same city the Republicans had used. Not only did the parties ape each other in national-committee formation and convention operations, but in 1884 they conducted their major activities in exactly the same place! The Mugwumps sent a contingent of their own to this second Chicago convention, hoping to sway undecided delegates to their first choice, Cleveland. Again, their direct impact on the result remains doubtful, but they felt they should try. They were playing for high stakes. If the candidate they eventually settled on did not win, they would be totally disgraced.

The Democratic convention got under way on Tuesday, July 8, exactly five weeks after the Republicans had convened. On the first day, the Tammany Braves lost their last chance to free themselves from the unit rule. Cleveland's bitter enemy Tom Grady proposed a resolution that essentially would have outlawed the procedure. If the national convention approved Grady's resolution, it would overrule the New York convention's instructions and permit Cleveland's opponents to express their opinions when the balloting began. After a lengthy debate, the resolution came to a vote, only to suffer defeat by a tally of 463 to 332. The numbers are somewhat misleading, however, since Manning, as chairman of the New York delegation, cast a unit-ruled seventy-two votes against the resolution. Its failure was not surprising. The unit rule represented a long-standing tradition in the Democratic party. Since the party also traditionally insisted that a two-thirds majority was necessary to nominate, the unit rule proved useful in creating large blocs of votes. Without it, a conclusion might never be reached.

Democratic conventions have often been rowdy, as witness 1968. The one in 1884 was no exception. The Democrats' feeling that they had an excellent chance to win buoyed their spirits, and exuberance and gaiety sparked the convention proceedings. The Democrats also concerned themselves less with formalities than did the Republicans and so began the nominating process while their resolutions committee remained locked in debate. Unlike the Republicans who had ruled that all speeches for a given candidate must be made consecutively, at the Democratic convention, the roll of the states prevailed, and a delegate could take the rostrum only upon the call of his own state's name, either to nominate a new man or to second an earlier nomination. This method of operation had the advantage of keeping many candidates' names alive throughout the proceedings. During the final minutes of this lengthy nomination process, the convention's most famous interchange took place. Responding to the call for Wisconsin, General Edward S. Bragg went to the platform. He noted that the men in his state supported Cleveland because "They love him, gentlemen, and they respect him, not only for himself, for his character, for his integrity and judgment and iron will, but they love him most for the enemies he has made." Tom Grady broke in to rebut this slur upon him and his fellows, but the majority of the Democrats, with whom Tammany was far from popular, gave it a spirited reception. The Mugwumps exactly shared Bragg's feelings.

The ethics of a convention's selecting a candidate before announcing its platform may be questionable, but, pragmatically, this practice helped move events along. The delay in the resolutions committee underlined a significant difference between the parties. The Republicans had scarcely noticed the adoption of their platform, concentrating their attention instead on nominees. The Democrats, on the other hand, devoted far more attention to their statement of resolves than to the Presidential candidate himself. When the resolutions committee finally presented its report, it became clear that customs duties had caused the delay. The Republicans had approved an unremarkable tariff plank committed to correcting inadequacies, meaning simply that the party intended to leave the existing high rates in operation. The Democrats could arrive at no such easy agreement. During the preceding spring, Democrats in the House of Representatives their party controlled had engaged in an inconclusive struggle over tariff reform. They had lost any chance of making changes in the rates when Democratic protectionists had voted with Republicans to kill a reform bill. The most outspoken of the Democratic protectionists, Representative Samuel J. Randall of Pennsylvania, derived his political support from industrial workers convinced that high duties guaranteed them high wages. A larger faction within the party followed the lead of Kentucky's

John G. Carlisle, currently Speaker of the House. Carlisle epito-
mized the low-tariff stance most Americans associated with the
Democratic party. A third group, which eventually had its way,
suggested that the Democrats should ignore their differences and
write out any tariff plank that would ensure a Democratic victory.

The resulting compromise pledged the Democratic party "to
revise the tariff in a spirit of fairness to all interests." No one
could argue with that. The plank also reiterated the argument
that high wages depended upon high tariffs, but concluded that
rates should be adjusted to reduce surplus revenues. A protectionist critic on the resolutions committee, former Governor
Ben Butler of Massachusetts, noted that the ambiguous plank
was "a mongrel resolution . . . which meant anything or nothing
as one chose to construct it." That was precisely the result most
Democrats desired, and the delegates overwhelmingly rejected
Butler's proposed alterations. The Democratic compromise left
the two parties with almost identical tariff planks, except that the
Democratic one was slightly more fuzzy. On almost every other
issue the two parties' sets of resolutions were virtually interchangeable.

The similarity of the platforms was comforting to the Mugwumps. They had justified their revolt from the Republican
party with the claim that the two parties had become virtually
identical. If the parties were identical, the Republican rebels
insisted, voters could and should select their Presidential candidate not on the basis of his party label, but for his personality,
attitudes, and especially his character. Since Blaine could just as
easily have run on the Democratic platform, the old arguments
concerning party loyalty and the Democratic threat to the Union
no longer applied. The Democrats had made themselves as
respectable as the Republicans.

Owing to delays in adopting the platform, the nomination
balloting began just before midnight on Thursday, the convention's third day. Cleveland's advocates had done their work
effectively; the Governor led on the first ballot with 392 votes,
more than twice the number granted Bayard, his nearest rival.
As soon as some of the other eight candidates dropped out of
the running, once delegates had fulfilled their obligations to

favorite sons, Cleveland would gain a clear majority. Having cast his state's seventy-two unit-ruled votes for the Governor, Manning devoted his attention to making sure that Cleveland's votes reached the necessary two-thirds mark. A most significant case of bargaining involved Pennsylvania Representative and favorite son, Samuel J. Randall, hastily called to Chicago, where he approved the transfer of his sixty protectionist votes to the obvious favorite.

During the night many other deals were concluded, among them a scheme to pack the galleries with men paid to shout for Indiana's Thomas A. Hendricks, Tilden's running mate in 1876. This plan went into operation without much success the following morning, during the second and final roll call. Cleveland ended this second round with 475 votes, more than three times Bayard's total and well ahead of third-running Hendricks. The convention's rules permitted a delegation to alter its vote before the results became official. Cleveland emerged from the ensuing melée of vote-changing with a winning total of 683 votes out of 820. Hendricks generously proposed unanimous endorsement for Cleveland and, later in the day, was rewarded with the Vice-Presidential nomination. He was not pleased to be running second again, although the gesture did resurrect the Old Ticket of 1876, which diehard Democrats claimed had won, with Tilden, a Reform Governor of New York, at the head and Hendricks as his running mate.

The result hardly surprised those outside the convention. The Democrats generally expected to win the election, although some of them worried about running the obscure Cleveland against one of the most widely known Republicans in the nation. Others considered the choice excellent, hoping that Tilden's heir would attract a winning majority. The Mugwumps could hardly have been more pleased: the Democratic party had chosen the man they themselves would have selected if they had been able to participate in the convention. Now they had a man to work for, and one with some chance of winning. They overlooked doubts about Cleveland's capabilities in joyously praising his nomination. His brief but honest record sufficiently assured the Mugwumps. As the *New York Times* noted just a day after the nomination, it had "closely watched the career of the candidate nominated at Chicago yesterday, and it has entire confidence in his probity, in his intelligence, and in his administrative ability. He ought to be the next President of the United States, and we believe he will be."

Not all the Independents who had rejected Blaine went over to Cleveland. Defection to the traditional enemy remained too much for some to swallow. Although the United States was basically operating under a two-party system in 1884, the lack of differences between the major party platforms encouraged several minor parties. Many a Republican who could not bring himself to support a Democratic nominee found an alternative in the Prohibition party. Temperance advocates had staged a disruptive demonstration at the Republican convention, hoping to have their plank added to the party's platform, but the party regulars chose to ignore this disturbance. When the Democratic party also remained hopelessly wet, the Prohibitionists determined to take independent action. They had run separate candidates in prior campaigns, never winning more than a tiny share of the votes. Once again, the Prohibitionists decided to run their own ticket.

Two Prohibition candidates eventually ran, but one attracted only a negligible number of votes. In late July, the regular Prohibition party held its convention and, for once, selected a surprisingly strong, nationally-known candidate. John P. St. John had recently won the governorship of Kansas on a combined Prohibition and Republican platform. Although St. John was unquestionably honest and qualified, the parochial nature of his platform frightened off many who might have swung his way. It represented dedication to an ideal, however, so many of those who could not stomach Blaine did end up supporting the Prohibition party. As the race heated up in the fall, St. John began to canvass for votes from the sympathetic Midwest and in New York State itself. The regular Republicans protested his actions, acting as though someone had cheated them out of the support they deserved from temperance men. But, by ignoring the issue, they had alienated prohibition voters just as surely as they lost others by sidestepping the Independent Republican complaints. On election day, St. John ran up an impressive total of over 25,000 votes in the pivotal state of New York, a tremendous increase over the 1880 Prohibition ticket's 1500.

While the Republicans suffered from a pygmy Prohibition attack, the Democrats had to counter the thrusts of an enemy of their own. Benjamin F. Butler had followed a most erratic political course. In the 1850's he had been a Democratic representative and senator from Massachusetts. A dedicated Unionist, he rose to the rank of major-general during the Civil War. As the Union general in charge of the occupation of New Orleans, Butler had made lifelong enemies in the South. After the war, he had developed into one of the most vociferous of the Radical Republicans, capping his career in the House of Representatives by serving as a prosecuting attorney during President Johnson's impeachment trial. When the Democrats swept the elections of 1874, Butler lost his seat. Never popular with the conservative elements in the Republican party, Butler opportunistically began relying upon Greenback supporters. He won a seat in the House as a Greenbacker in 1878 and from there made the short jump back into the Democratic party. His Greenback, Labor, and Democratic supporters formed a coalition effective enough in the Democratic year of 1882 to boost the erstwhile Radical into the governor's chair in Massachusetts. Although he lost the office the following year, Butler claimed to be a power of sorts in the Democratic party.

The Democrats were reluctant to welcome him, although his successful restructuring of Massachusetts political forces made him appear to be a friend of the workingman. In the spring of 1884, his reputation attracted a newly formed splinter group, called the Antimonopoly party. The title told all. The disgruntled party members hated the rich, and they wanted the federal government to step in and actively discourage the formation of powerful business combinations. They settled upon Butler as a Presidential candidate simply because he was the only famous man around who had allied himself with labor. Butler delayed accepting the nomination, not wanting to commit himself until he had seen what other opportunities might come his way.

The Greenback-Labor party, which had helped Butler in Massachusetts, also held a Presidential convention in 1884, nominating the ex-Governor. Coupled with his Antimonopoly bid, the Greenback nomination gave Butler the semblance of strong labor support. The General still refused to accept, however, hoping to parlay these two splinter-party nominations into something more valuable at the upcoming Democratic convention. As a member of the Democratic resolutions committee, Butler appeared on the floor of the convention only after the platform's completion. By that time, all the nominating speeches were over. Butler vainly hoped that his labor support would win him the regular party's nomination, but the Democrats totally ignored the political renegade. In the end, he had no choice but to accept the splinter nominations and try to undercut Cleveland. Charles Dana's *New York Sun* broke with the Democratic party and became Butler's most enthusiastic press supporter—indeed, virtually the only one. As the campaign advanced, unreliable reporters circulated the rumor that the Blaineites were underwriting Butler's candidacy. Whether it was true or not, the extra nominee caused Cleveland's managers a great deal of discomfort.

8. The Campaign

Blaine! Blaine! James G. Blaine! Continental liar from the State of Maine!

Ma, Ma, where's my pa? Gone to the White House, ha, ha, ha!

—Campaign slogans (1884)

With all the candidates nominated, campaign activities could begin in earnest. Having already decided not to form a party of their own, the Mugwumps had to devise an alternative organization to maximize their influence. After the Democrats selected Cleveland, the Mugwumps intended to announce their support for him in the most dramatic manner possible. Since three of New York's formerly Republican daily newspapers and three of its nationally circulated weeklies were praising Cleveland to the skies, that city seemed the logical location for such a demonstration. The June 17 meeting in New York had proposed a second gathering in July to announce and solidify the Mugwump position.

This second meeting began to resemble a convention in size and scope. Being otherwise unemployed at the time, Carl Schurz coordinated the plans for the meeting. He sent out invitations to prominent Independents, and more than four hundred of them, including a contingent of fifty from Massachusetts, assembled on July 22, 1884. Curtis presided over the proceedings, and Massachusetts lawyer Moorfield Storey opened the round of speeches. The Mugwumps agreed to support Cleveland but voted to ignore his running mate, Hendricks, whom they considered as reprehensible as Republican Vice-Presidential candidate Logan. They reaffirmed their decision not to form a third party, but at the same time to avoid becoming a slavish adjunct to the Democratic party. The Mugwumps intended to remain independent of all party ties during the months to come, an inevitable decision in view of their dismay about partisan tactics. They well knew that the Democrats were not paragons of political virtue, and they meant to conduct any joint actions with them on a very informal basis. The Democratic party happened to have chosen a candidate the Mugwumps liked, but the rest of its partisan paraphernalia held no attraction for them.

To publicize their intentions, the members of the conference approved a strongly worded resolution. The Mugwump declaration of principles, later printed and distributed by the New York committee, announced that the rebels had decided to break their party ties because

The paramount issue of the Presidential election of this year is moral rather than political. It concerns the national honor and character, and honesty of administration rather than general policies of government, upon which the platforms of the two parties do not essentially differ. . . . In a time of profound peace at home and abroad the most threatening national peril is an insidious political corruption, a mercenary and demoralizing spirit and tendency.

In the absence of grave government responsibilities, the Mugwumps felt that the parties should devote their energies to reforming themselves. As a first step, they intended to help elect Cleveland, a man not yet associated with the coarser elements of his party.

Having met to announce their support for the Democratic candidate and, of course, to reassure one another of the wisdom of this stand, the conference delegates had fulfilled their primary function. Directing their emotions and feelings into substantive channels would be more difficult. Never intending to merge with the Democratic party, the Independent bolters wanted to develop an alternative that would enable them to retain their essential Republicanism despite their abrupt divergence from the mainstream of the party. They settled on the expedient of the forming of political-action clubs throughout the Northeast and in a few Western cities as well. In the vicinity of the central New York headquarters, clubs appeared in Connecticut, Rhode Island, New Jersey, and Massachusetts. Further afield, Mugwump organizations of one sort or another sprang up in Pennsylvania, Ohio, Indiana, Illinois, Wisconsin, and Iowa. Some of these clubs catered to specific interest groups, such as the Cleveland and Hendricks Business Men's Association of New York. Others, like the Massachusetts Reform Club, were older, established organizations that had been converted to the new cause.

The leading national group, the New York Independent National Committee, established its headquarters at 35 Nassau Street. While Curtis was its nominal head, young activists like R. R. Bowker and Horace E. Deming did most of the committee's routine work. With the $25,000 the committee managed to raise during the campaign, it published pamphlets, sent out speakers, and helped other Mugwumps to organize local clubs. A similar organization appeared in Boston, headed by George Fred Williams. Chicago Mugwumps, too, had their own central headquarters for publicity and pamphleteering. Beyond the strong personal ties many of the members felt for one another, there was little unity among the various regional groups. They willingly shared ideas and speakers, but they never developed a central leadership.

The Independent newspapers and journals did yeoman work. Without a solidly committed corps of journalists to spread its ideas, the Mugwump movement might never have come into being at all. Totally committed to Cleveland, the Mugwump journals went to great lengths to defend him from every slur and to commend each glimmering of reform sentiment he exhibited. Sometimes they outdid even the most partisan Democrat journals in lauding the candidate. Whenever a Mugwump felt the outlook depressed or his commitment flagging, he could turn to the current issue of *Harper's Weekly*, the *Nation*, or any of the daily Independent papers to find soul-stirring reassurance.

In their energetic promotion of Cleveland and their unstinting criticism of Blaine, the Mugwump journalists sometimes exceeded the bounds of objectivity. If they avoided telling outright lies, they were guilty at least of telling only part of the truth. Seldom content with straightforward statements of fact, the Mugwumps interpreted and twisted their stories to suit themselves. Editorializing about Blaine in late September, for example, the *New York Times* stated, "There is no speculation which he can resist; but, rich as he is, he has never earned money by any visible business or profession." A few days later the *New York Herald* contended that "Mr. Blaine cares nothing about the tariff. What he wants is the maintenance of exorbitant, needless and burdensome taxes as a huge corruption fund." Fortunately, the Mugwump press was not punished for its warping of the news. Once during the campaign, Blaine did initiate a libel suit against an Indianapolis Democratic newspaper that had dredged up a fraudulent story about his son. But many Americans considered it somewhat unsportsmanlike to go that far, given the generally high emotional level of political rhetoric at the time.

It might appear that the Mugwump publicists had abandoned their self-proclaimed idealism, but they would have denied such a charge. The Independents acted as though they were fighting a battle against one of the most serious threats the nation had ever faced. In such a struggle they could justifiably use almost any weapon. They generally limited their attention to Blaine's public record, but they felt free to editorialize any way they could to make him appear morally depraved. Consequently they were doubly chagrined and embarrassed when a damaging story spread about their own candidate. They tried to gloss over the news by arguing that Cleveland's had been a private misadventure which in no way affected his fitness for public office, but the Halpin Scandal obviously shook their confidence to its foundations.

A Buffalo newspaper first circulated the report on the very day,

July 22, that the Independents approved their resolution pompously decreeing that the paramount issue was moral rather than political. Sifting through all the speculation and rumors embellishing the story, it is clear that twelve years earlier, in 1872, Cleveland had assumed the responsibility for having fathered an illegitimate son. The boy's mother, Mrs. Maria Halpin, had made the allegations. Although Mrs. Halpin had been on intimate terms with a number of men, Cleveland, the only bachelor involved, had seen to ensuring the child's welfare. Eventually one of his well-to-do acquaintances adopted the boy. Cleveland was still a bachelor in 1884, and unscrupulous journalists exploited the Halpin story to create an image of the Governor as a libertine. Rumors circulated that he had been publicly drunk and that women of ill repute frequented the executive mansion in Albany.

Needless to say, these revelations rocked the resolution of the Mugwumps, who had been praising Cleveland as a model of uprightness. His steadfast reaction, however, helped to recoup some of their faith. Rather than attempt to weasel out of the charges or make a dramatic gesture as Blaine had done in 1876 during the Mulligan Letters episode, Cleveland requested his friends simply to "tell the truth." In this way, he reassured the Mugwumps of his basic honesty and at the same time quelled those rumors that lacked foundation. The Mugwumps grudgingly admitted that their man had been guilty of private moral lapses, which, at least, had ended some time in the past. They took elaborate pains to convince themselves and others that Cleveland had since become the soul of propriety. At one point, they sent the Reverend James Freeman Clarke to interview the candidate. A respected cleric, representative of the puritanical Boston code of ethics, Clarke pronounced Cleveland cured of his past indiscretions. (The endorsement of another minister, Henry Ward Beecher, proved embarrassing to the Mugwumps, for Beecher himself had once suffered public mortification as a result of adulterous exploits.)

Many critics considered the Mugwumps' attitude toward the scandal inconsistent with their protestations of commitment to ideals. Indeed, the story led some of them to shift their support to St. John, who did not even drink. But most of them determined to stick with their original choice, claiming to care less about his youthful flings than about his current attitude toward public office. Cleveland had thus far proved to be virtually above criticism in his conduct of public responsibilities. One of his campaign managers suggested the slogan "Public office is a public trust," and the Governor adopted it as his motto. This attitude corresponded exactly with that of the Mugwumps, who were encouraged by it to overlook his private life.

Cleveland's public image changed scarcely at all during the campaign. He remained hard at work in Albany, refusing to abandon his duties as governor. He made only two major campaign appearances after his nomination, one at his New Jersey birthplace and the other in his home town, Buffalo. Otherwise he seemed almost oblivious to the campaign activities that swirled about him. The American people learned little more about him as a man or as a politician in the course of the canvass for votes. He approached national issues very cautiously, fully cognizant of his own lack of experience in dealing with them. On tariff matters particularly, he freely admitted his ignorance, allowing the ambiguous Democratic platform to represent his own views.

Lacking more knowledge about Cleveland, the newspapers were forced to rehash old issues and analyze his brief record as governor. The Mugwumps stoutly claimed to be completely satisfied with his public record. He had used his veto power rather freely but apparently only out of solid conviction of the correctness of his actions. He had approved and implemented the New York Civil Service Act, but then again, President Arthur had done as much at the federal level. Among those who were uneasy about Cleveland's enigmatic personality were some influential Mugwump leaders. Behind their public façade of total commitment to and satisfaction with the man, they were writing one another in an effort to determine his true attitude toward civil-service reform.

By October, this carefully masked uneasiness had grown to such an extent that even George William Curtis wanted clarification. He wrote to the Governor asking exactly how he proposed to deal with the spoils if elected. Cleveland sent a comforting reply on October 24, in which he announced in favor of the retention of officeholders in positions he deemed non-political—in other words, those, excluding his immediate advisers, who dealt with routine administrative matters. He added that he considered removals for political reasons unjustifiable and believed that any civil servant who had attended to his official duties and had not used his office simply as a party sinecure should be retained. This position implied, of course, a subjective assessment of the officeholders' capabilities by the President or a subordinate. Cleveland deliberately left himself this loophole, for he did not want to be trapped into restrictions upon his appointive power if he won. But the Governor's response reassured his Mugwump backers. The affair indicates, however, how strongly the Mugwumps disapproved of Blaine, for they had gone all out to support a man whose attitude toward their pet reform they did not even know. Furthermore, regardless of how sincerely Cleveland supported reform, his fellow Democrats would subject him to tremendous pressure on the question of patronage.

The army of Democratic partisans who would accompany Cleveland into office gave many a Mugwump pause. While the reformers had been decrying machines and corruption in their own party, the Democratic party had employed many of the methods the Mugwumps considered reprehensible in the Republicans. The current Southern Democratic leadership represented the same sort of men whom some of the older Independent Republicans had thoroughly despised before the war. The conservative Democratic leaders in the Northeast appeared to be sound on economic issues, and their tendency to support low tariffs appealed to many Independents, but even there, the presence of wily political manipulators like Manning in the forefront of Cleveland's campaign boded ill for the future.

To New York City Mugwumps, Tammany Hall was the most notorious example of Democratic unsuitability. Unfortunately, any rational political assessment indicated that Cleveland would need Tammany votes to win in November. An acceptable solution developed when Tammany Hall held its convention in September. Much as he disliked the Governor, Tammany chief John Kelly recognized the importance of a Democratic victory for the entire party. He also realized that if such a victory occurred and he had failed to commit himself to Cleveland, the national party would completely cut him out of all reward. Kelly's political self-interest overrode his personal distaste for Cleveland, and he decided to have the Tammany convention endorse the regular Democratic nominee. State Senator Tom Grady had enough standing within the machine to disagree with the boss, and he did so dramatically. When Tammany's general membership voted overwhelmingly to line up behind Cleveland, Grady stalked out of the convention with many of his friends. They worked energetically for Butler throughout the fall. Kelly himself was rumored to have helped stage the rebellion, for the Grady pullout left Kelly safely in the party, while his machine had symbolically rejected its candidate.

Cleveland's campaign managers did little to reassure Mugwumps concerned about his party's influence on him. The Democratic party had selected William H. Barnum as national committee chairman, in recognition of his willingness to contribute heavily to the party. Barnum was reputed to have bought a U.S. Senate seat in Connecticut a few years earlier. Little more than a figurehead in 1884, Barnum left most campaign decisions to the extremely able Arthur Pue Gorman, who had used the spoils system in his home state of Maryland to propel himself into the Senate as well. Officially charged with coordinating all 1884 Democratic congressional campaigns, Gorman superintended the Cleveland canvass at the same time. He leaned heavily upon Manning and William C. Whitney, a wealthy Democratic leader who had risen to prominence in the County Democracy, Tammany's rival in New York City. Whitney's connections to the Standard Oil fortune enabled him to serve as the party's leading fund raiser. None of these men was idealistically motivated, nor would the Mugwumps have considered voting for any of them. In the rough and tumble struggle for the Presidency, however, professional political managers often proved more vital than attractive candidates. At least the Democratic leaders were no worse than those who handled Blaine's campaign.

Another wealthy figurehead, B. F. Jones, a Pennsylvania steel magnate, headed the Republican hierarchy, serving for precisely the same reasons and about as effectively as Barnum did for the Democrats. As Gorman's counterpart, the Blaineites relied upon Stephen B. Elkins, the epitome of the successful Republican spoilsman. The peripatetic Elkins intermittently represented Missouri, New Mexico Territory, and West Virginia, finishing off his political career in the early twentieth century as a Senator from the latter state. Rumored to be one of the leading figures behind the recently publicized Star Route Frauds, he possessed outstanding abilities as a machine politician. He reportedly based his plans for 1884 on the proposition that political success was "largely a question of finance," and he pinpointed New York, Indiana, and West Virginia as his major targets. In New York he was supposed to have negotiated a secret arrangement with John Kelly, and in Indiana he hoped to buy enough floaters to provide a winning majority. Since money was essential to the success of his plans, Elkins urged the party's many friends to contribute generously.

The gradual shift toward a reformed civil service increased the Republicans' difficulties in levying their demands upon federal officeholders. Recent legislation forbade the practice of deducting party contributions from pay checks, so Republican managers devised ingenious schemes to replace that older, guaranteed method. For example, they established an office with tellers and cashiers near the Treasury Building in Washington to keep track of officeholders' contributions. The Mugwump press kept up a running criticism of these schemes, and it proudly reported that income from such sources had dropped off significantly. The alternative, which eventually more than replaced the lost contributions from civil servants, was to convince businessmen that they should support the Republican party for selfish reasons. Both sides developed persuasive arguments along these lines, however. In 1884, the two major parties collected almost equal amounts from outside contributors, once again showing how closely they were balanced. Many businessmen considered a Democratic contribution a wise investment, as the party appeared to have a good chance of winning.

Meanwhile, Blaine ignored the more mundane aspects of the campaign, trusting Elkins and others to do what they could through normal partisan procedures. The Plumed Knight took orders from no one. In this one respect, the two candidates acted quite similarly. Each let his managers and partisans do the bulk of the work.

Cursory perusal of the Mugwump literature churned out in 1884 might convince the reader that Blaine was the most corrupt man in the United States. Day after day, articles and editorials hammered away at the same themes: Blaine was dishonest, self-seeking, and probably criminal. A more thorough analysis of Mugwump reporting would reveal how few facts underlay these assertions. Obviously Blaine had consorted with and accepted assistance from machine leaders in his party. But so had Cleveland. Nevertheless, the Mugwumps felt that Blaine's longer association with these types had made him more likely to have succumbed to their brand of dishonesty. Blaine knew he could not wipe the slate clean; his record had been public for years. While a good many Americans, including a vast majority of Republicans, did not consider it a bad record, the Mugwumps chose to subject it to the worst possible interpretation.

The Mulligan letters remained fundamental to Mugwump propaganda. Already thoroughly discussed and investigated, they provided the Independent Republican rebels with their one tangible shred of evidence. Trying him almost solely on this evidence, the Mugwumps convicted Blaine of the crime of public dishonesty. Ambiguities in the letters themselves left them open to a variety of interpretations, however, and a good many honest Republicans disagreed with the bolters' contention that they proved Blaine guilty of wrongdoing. The Mulligan revelations had been public knowledge for eight years, and during that period, nothing had appeared to alter decisions already made.

Fortunately for the Mugwump campaign, some new information came to light a couple of months before the election when James Mulligan contacted Moorfield Storey and James Freeman Clarke. Mulligan told the Mugwumps that he had rifled Warren Fisher's letter files and assembled a second batch of evidence.

Upon the predictable advice of Storey and Clarke, Mulligan turned these new revelations over to the *Boston Journal* for publication in mid-September. The Mugwumps enthusiastically sifted through the new correspondence and discovered that it did little either to confirm or disprove their original interpretations. They enjoyed playing around with a new set of letters, however, and one in particular fascinated them.

Blaine had written this controversial letter on April 16, 1876, while the House was investigating his conduct. With the letter Blaine had enclosed a draft that he wanted Fisher to copy and send back to him. It would have Fisher state that he had no knowledge of any dishonest dealings involving Blaine and that he and Blaine had acted strictly within accepted moral codes. Fisher had ignored the request to help clear Blaine's name. Instead, he had given Mulligan access to his files and allowed the secretary to go to Washington to testify against the ex-Speaker of the House. Fisher had also ignored Blaine's final injunction, "Burn this letter."

The Mugwumps revelled in this new intelligence, pointing out that a man with nothing to hide need not request an exonerating statement from a correspondent. Furthermore, the covering letter revealed Blaine in a weak, pleading position. The new letters may have converted a few additional Republicans to Mugwumpery, but they served mainly to boost morale in the rebel camp. Mulligan's actions caught the Republicans unaware, but Blaine insisted that nothing in the new batch of letters impugned his reputation. He even suggested that every Republican read the letters so as to learn how unjustified were the Mugwump assertions. A few weeks later, however, the opposition press gleefully reported that a Republican speaker had roundly criticized a hawker selling copies of the letters at a partisan gathering. The Mugwumps regarded the publicizing of what they considered new evidence of Blaine's corruption as one of their leading contributions to the campaign. The letters definitely spiced up the race, and they gave the Democrats a delightful slogan. "Burn this letter" began to appear on posters and banners throughout the country.

The Mugwumps' enthusiastic criticism of Blaine was based on scant evidence, but they did not care; they were less concerned with proving Blaine's guilt than with preventing his election. Whether guilty or innocent of malfeasance, Blaine remained closely identified with elements in the Republican party that the rebels abhorred. Many Mugwumps personally hated the man, it is true, but beyond that lay their disgust with his associates and his long-range policies and their anger at the gradual transformation of their party into a selfish organization.

The 1884 Mugwump revolt encouraged the natural trend toward concentration on the personalities of the candidates. With the party platforms all but interchangeable, differences in the nominees' characters provided the most reasonable basis for choosing between them. Most voters, of course, would follow traditional party loyalties and vote as they always had. The Independents, the undecided, and the uncommitted became increasingly concerned with the personal emphasis of the campaign. Each candidate had his liabilities. Blaine's character was so well known that a fully documented rebuttal was available to counter every laudatory statement about him. Cleveland's obscurity left him open to speculative criticism and equally speculative praise. Neither man's attitudes on particular issues aroused much attention.

Among the few nonpersonal issues that stimulated some interest during the campaign, the tariffs predominated. For different reasons, both the Mugwumps and the Democrats tried to say nothing about them. Both took delight in observing Blaine's managers' assiduous attempt to encourage discussion about customs duties. Since Blaine was the nation's leading advocate of protection, wherever he went, the tariff issue inevitably followed. He had originally intended to keep the Democrats on the defensive with the issue, counting on avid support from both management and labor. A preponderance of Democratic leaders favored lower rates, and if Blaine's onslaught had successfully forced them into a public defense of their positions, the many protectionist Mugwumps would have become extremely unhappy. To pre-empt the issue from the Republicans, the Mugwumps found a method of concentrating on the prevailing tariff system that tied in with their major criticism of Blaine.

The bolters knew full well that the surplus of federal revenues embarrassed protectionists. The Mugwumps argued that high revenues encouraged governmental waste and inefficiency, which, in turn, promoted corruption as lobbyists flooded Washington, trying to persuade legislators to fund their pet programs. Thus, while one set of favor seekers urged ever higher tariff rates, another tried to exploit the resulting surplus revenues for their own purposes. Honest civil servants and legislators were trapped in the cross fire of these demands. Therefore, some Mugwumps contended, a reduction of the tariffs would help to clean up government and end partisan corruption. The protectionist Mugwumps, on the other hand, found comfort in the Democratic platform's failure to call for drastic reductions in the prevailing rates.

With the exception of sporadic discussion of tariffs during the campaign of 1884 both parties deliberately ignored the nation's economic troubles, for which neither had a solution. The people's needs ran secondary to the parties' selfish desires. Party procedures were so well established, however, that the campaign developed an exciting tempo despite its failure to encompass meaningful issues. Even the self-righteous Mugwumps joined in.

Circulation figures for the Mugwump press give some indication of the interest the campaign aroused. Despite their revolutionary stands, both the *Times* and the *Post* managed to maintain sales of about 90,000 issues each per day during the fall of 1884. The *Times* would lose about half its readership after the election, however, showing the severe economic consequences of its Mugwump defection. The more popular *New York Herald* averaged about 160,000 readers a day, and the illustrated weeklies, *Harper's* and *Puck*, sold approximately 125,000 copies of each issue. In the New York City area alone, then, the Mugwump journals' circulation ran around a half million throughout the canvass for voters. Even allowing for some duplication of readership, it appears that the reform message reached a large number of voters in the city. Mugwump journals did equally well in other areas during the campaign.

A problem facing all the newspapers, regardless of party affiliation, was the paucity of real news. A cooling-off period followed the flurry of interest the conventions had induced. Not until early September did the race heat up in anticipation of elections in the several states that chose local officials before the first Tuesday of November, the Presidential election day. As they do today, political pundits tried to read the results of these early contests as indicators of national trends. No one seriously expected the Maine and Vermont elections in September to reveal anything but strong Republican sentiment. Since the Vermont Democrats had thrown up only token opposition, the Mugwumps cheered when Republican candidates in that state won with 10 per cent fewer votes than they had polled in the previous Presidential year. The rebels were inevitably disappointed in Maine, where favorite-son Blaine's presence in the Presidential race aided his party. The popular Republican incumbents in his state easily won re-election.

Far more significant than these predictable Republican victories would be the results of mid-October elections in Ohio and West Virginia. The Republicans hoped to capture both states, although Ohio had gone Democratic in 1882 and West Virginia normally fell into the solid Democratic South. No one could confidently predict the outcome in either state, so both the Democrats and Republicans energetically pursued their orthodox, though not necessarily honest, methods of rounding up votes. The Mugwumps did their share as well, although they never hoped for much from Ohio.

Lacking a machine to work for them, the Mugwumps did the next best thing by sending Carl Schurz on a speaking tour through the Midwest. At times, in fact, Schurz appeared to be a one-man movement. He had delivered a penetrating analysis of the Mulligan letters at an address in Brooklyn in August, and he used it as a framework for his speeches on tour. He spoke twenty-two times in Ohio, and went as far west as Milwaukee to stir up German-speaking voters. Schurz accepted some expense money from local admirers, but he himself defrayed a good part of the costs of the tour. He earned enthusiastic responses in the Midwest, but few Mugwumps followed his example. The Mugwump press avidly praised his efforts, while the Republican journals ridiculed them.

Although the over-all impact of Schurz's tour remained subject to question, he did take credit for forcing Blaine to campaign for himself. The Republican Presidential candidate had devoted a good deal of attention to Maine's state elections, and, having succeeded handsomely, decided to conduct a speaking tour of the West. The Mugwumps were overjoyed. They felt sure that Blaine would never have considered a tiring personal tour had their efforts not frightened him into it. For weeks, Thomas Nast's cartoons in *Harper's Weekly* had been depicting the Plumed Knight as a traveling salesman, wearing a beaver hat decorated with a bedraggled white feather and carrying a carpetbag upon which a variety of uncomplimentary legends appeared, as if to illustrate the bill of goods Blaine was trying to sell the voters. The cartoonist could hardly have been more pleased when the great personage took to the road, bringing Nast's caricature to life.

Blaine decided on his own to make the tour, although he did it after consulting with his managers. For a variety of reasons, Republican prospects were far from bright, and it seemed only logical for the party to put its most effective spokesman to work. Only two other Presidential candidates had ever toured in their own behalf, Stephen Douglas desperately in 1860, and Horace Greeley hopelessly in 1872. It was more customary for the nominee to remain aloof and silent, permitting others to beat the bushes, as Cleveland was doing more out of temperament than out of respect for tradition.

Blaine began his travels on September 17, whistle-stopping through New York and Massachusetts before moving west to Pennsylvania, West Virginia, Ohio, Michigan, Indiana, and Illinois. He did not return home to Maine until election day, November 4. Several persons accompanied him throughout, while local Republican notables joined his entourage whenever he passed through their home stamping grounds. His incredible memory for names and faces did much to heighten the impact of his tour, and his oratorical skill prevented all but a few minor slips. Unlike Schurz, Blaine did not repeat a stock address over and over again, preferring instead to speak almost extemporaneously whenever he stopped.

Blaine's tour focused attention on the Ohio and West Virginia elections in October. Republican publicists touted Blaine as Garfield's heir, although that Ohio favorite son had managed to carry the state by a plurality of only 19,000 votes in 1880. In an extremely close finish, Republican candidates did carry the governorship and other major prizes by about 10,000 votes out of 800,000 cast. The Republicans claimed to have reversed the Democratic trend of 1882, while the Mugwumps considered the halving of Garfield's plurality quite significant. Perhaps the most honest assessment of the Ohio result was that it did not significantly alter the national outlook. A Democratic sweep in West Virginia's state elections, held the same day, proved equally unenlightening.

The campaign's final three weeks evoked considerable excitement, for no one could be sure how the race would end on November 4. Blaine continued to tour the Midwest, spending some time in Indiana, although bribing that state's huge floating voter class would probably have proved more effective. Republican partisan W. W. Dudley, one of the many civil servants who participated actively in the campaign, helped to convince quite a few wavering voters. Dudley, head of the U.S. Pensions Bureau, led a group of roving agents to the doubtful states of Ohio and Indiana, where they quickly and generously settled outstanding veterans' claims on the spot, making it clear where the veterans' true interests lay. Republican-sponsored veterans' claims would provoke a flood of Presidential vetoes once Cleveland took office.

Blaine spent a brief period in company with Vice-Presidential candidate Logan, whose veteran-supported Stalwart machine in Illinois looked invincible. Logan and Blaine disliked each other, and the General apparently did not appreciate the Plumed Knight's incursion into his home state. Wherever Blaine went, questions arose about his alleged dishonesty. Alone, Logan had managed to ignore such innuendos and devote his attention to the old, safe Civil War issues. Blaine, too, enjoyed waving the Bloody Shirt, which he did with increasing vigor once West Virginia had aligned herself with the Southern Democratic bloc. Some thoughtless Republicans attempted to criticize Cleveland's lack of a war record, but Blaine had also avoided military service by hiring a substitute. Worse still, Blaine's stand-in was later imprisoned for selling forged deferment papers. At last, therefore, the American people managed to get through a political campaign with a minimum of attention to the war issues. Blaine fatefully decided to break his trip home with a stop in New York City. The nation's leading metropolis contained the most insistent Mugwump propagandists along with enthusiastic political activists of all sorts. New York's thirty-six electoral votes were crucial and the state's party balance close. Since Blaine's tour had been favorably received in the West, worried Republican managers requested that he add New York to his itinerary in the closing week of the campaign.

Blaine and his advisers knew that the Mugwump defection would hurt them in New York, so the Republicans turned to an alternative. The Irish-Americans who proliferated in the city had traditionally served as the backbone for Democratic machines. Tom Grady's walkout from Tammany Hall had already wooed a few of the Irish away from Cleveland, and Butler's guerrilla attack on Democratic labor support had further weakened him. Blaine determined to undermine still further Cleveland's support among the millions of Irish-American voters. The Republican candidate felt that he possessed the proper credentials to attract this ethnic vote, for his father's family had come from northern Ireland, his mother was an Irish Catholic, and he had a sister who was a nun. Furthermore, Blaine had a record of strong opposition to England. As Cleveland had taken no stand on foreign policy, the Republicans tried to depict him as pro-British. Blaine's spokesmen rang all the changes on the theme, even claiming that the free-trade notions prevalent in the Democratic party represented a British plot to destroy the nation. Blaine's beachhead in the Irish community worried the Mugwumps, who knew that their own small contribution could never offset a substantial swing of the city's huge Irish population to Blaine.

A late campaign incident that involved a queer melding of these elements captured the nation's attention. On October 29, a party of clergymen arrived at Blaine's hotel in New York City to see the great man in person. The religious leaders were a mixed assemblage representing many faiths and degrees of bigotry. Their scheduled spokesman had been called out of town, so the leaderless group arbitrarily selected the oldest cleric among them, the Reverend Daniel Burchard, to greet the candidate. Blaine appeared on the stairs and listened politely, if disinterestedly, to Burchard's platitudes. Along the way, Presbyterian Burchard blurted out a pithy alliteration in reference to the Democratic party, calling it "the party of rum, Romanism, and rebellion."

Blaine failed to repudiate this slur upon the Catholics he had been endeavoring to placate. Meanwhile, a stenographer whom Democratic manager Gorman had sent to the meeting wrote out a verbatim report. Democratic and Mugwump propagandists capitalized on this slight to the Irish. Blaine later contended that he had not heard the offending words; otherwise he would naturally have refuted them. But the damage was done. Gorman and his fellows made sure that the slanderous phrase circulated widely in Democratic wards. They even sent postcards to local Catholic priests, hoping that they would mention the incident at their masses on the Sunday before the election. The episode occurred so late in the campaign that Blaine simply could not reverse the damage. After the election, the Republicans singled out the Burchard incident as the primary cause for their defeat. Nevertheless, Blaine did make serious inroads in traditionally Democratic Irish wards. How much better he might have done without Burchard's statement will never be known.

To finish off the disastrous day's activities, Blaine attended a posh fund-raising dinner organized by Cyrus Field at Delmonico's restaurant and attended by several of the wealthiest men in the nation. Blaine's magnetic presence among this coterie of moguls and the impassioned praise of the speakers should have been effective, but the session produced relatively little revenue. Many wealthy men had already carefully hedged their bets with donations to the Democrats, for the Republican outlook was none too promising.

Not only did the banquet fail to produce funds, it also aroused bad publicity. The following morning, the Democratic New York *World* published a front-page cartoon entitled "Belshazzaar's

Feast," showing Blaine and the other diners glutting themselves on a sumptuous meal while a starving family stood by, denied even the scraps of the repast. The Mugwumps roundly criticized Blaine's close association with moneyed rogues, noting that the banquet had come too late in the campaign for any of its proceeds to be used for honest purposes. Obviously, many of these last-minute contributions would fall into the hands of floaters paid to support Blaine. The Burchard incident and the Delmonico banquet gave the Mugwumps plenty to talk about in the campaign's final week.

9. The Election

The only hope of our opponents is in a fraudulent count in the country districts. Call to your assistance today vigilant and courageous friends, and see that every vote is honestly counted.

—Telegram sent to local Democratic officials in the name of New York State Democratic Committee Chairman DANIEL MANNING, November 5, 1884

On Tuesday, November 4, 1884, the voters went to the polls. Party machines in the cities and in rural areas brought all their influence to bear at the balloting stations. In tougher urban wards, partisan bullies hung around the polls, monitoring the activities of the electorate. They could easily keep track of how each man had voted since the secret ballot concept had not yet become popular in the United States. Individual voters obtained ballots from party officials or clipped them from newspapers. The ballots printed in the Mugwump papers listed only the Cleveland electors, while the *Tribune* and other Republican papers published Blaine's list.

In not a few cases, the votes cast in a district outnumbered the registered voters, so poll watchers had to invalidate some of the ballots. Partisans on both sides employed questionable techniques; both major parties were guilty of deceit and fraud. In the end, perhaps the scheming on all sides tended to cancel itself out. The existence of four tickets aggravated the normal election-day turmoil, particularly in New York State. Butler's support in urban Democratic wards did much to offset St. John's backing in rural Republican ones.

As long as the result remained unclear, even the most inconsequential of events seemed to assume a dramatic importance. For example, the Republicans claimed that the heavy rains which fell in upstate New York on election day literally dampened the enthusiasm of many of the Grand Old Party's supporters in outlying regions. At the same time, it interrupted telephone service to the executive mansion in Albany, cutting Cleveland off from any news for a time. He reportedly went to bed early, as did Blaine—the wisest course, since the final verdict remained unknown for several days.

Early returns suggested that Cleveland would win. As expected, he walked off with all 153 of the solid South's electoral votes. In addition he barely won Connecticut's six, Indiana's fifteen, and New Jersey's nine—an assured total of 183 electoral votes. Blaine appeared certain of capturing 182. Only New York's thirty-six votes remained in doubt, and there Cleveland seemed well in the lead. Ordinarily strong rural Republican constituencies had shown less than their usual enthusiasm for Blaine. Many Republican voters had obviously switched to St. John, and perhaps some had succumbed to Mugwump influences and turned to Cleveland. If this trend away from the Republican party had prevailed throughout the state, Cleveland would have ended up with a substantial majority. But late reports from the normally solid Democratic city wards showed a sloughing off of Democratic strength. Butler received many of the wayward votes, but Blaine also did well in the city. His missionary work among the Irish Catholics had proved effective despite the Burchard episode.

The Mugwump organizations had not intended to continue operating after November 4, and they had deliberately spent all their funds by that date in anticipation of closing down. Now the rebels, reopened their offices, determined to prevent Blaine from winning the long struggle on some technicality. Until the opposition conceded, no party organization intended to relax. The Democrats felt certain that they had won; the Republicans were less sure but still hopeful. Politicians who had planned on taking well-earned vacations and partisans who had been operating at a fever pitch for the last few days remained attentive. The people, too, became confused and uneasy. The newspapers did nothing to calm the situation.

The lack of conclusive results on Wednesday did not discourage the *Tribune* from magnanimously awarding New York to Blaine, thus enabling the paper to declare its man the winner. The Mugwump and Democratic press gave the Empire State to Cleveland with an estimated 10,000-vote plurality and proclaimed him the national victor. By Thursday, both sides had substantially toned down their claims, although the *Tribune* still claimed New York for Blaine. The Democrats and Mugwumps reduced their previous estimates considerably, stating that only about 2,500 votes appeared to separate the two major contenders, with Cleveland barely coming out on top in the state.

In an age without instantaneous mass-communication devices, newspaper offices became popular gathering places. Several journals set up big billboards outside their headquarters upon which they recorded the latest news. At the Associated Press offices, an especially unruly crowd collected in response to rumors that the owner of the news service, Jay Gould, had been manipulating returns. Infamous for his financial maneuverings, Gould also owned the Western Union organization, which telegraphed the returns to central locations. According to the prevalent gossip, Gould had been holding back results favorable to Cleveland and releasing only those that would make Blaine appear to be the winner. Meanwhile, as they were reputed to have done so effectively in 1876, Republican managers supposedly sent messages out to partisans in the field, indicating that if certain districts reported in a particular way, Blaine would win. Presumably, Republican-controlled canvassing boards in rural areas might then report in the suggested results, and Blaine would, in fact, be victorious. By Friday, the mob threat to Gould's offices was such that the Wall Street manipulator sent Cleveland a note congratulating him on his victory.

The Democrats had taken strong precautions to ensure the Governor's success. Analyzing early returns, Cleveland's managers realized that the New York result would be extraordinarily close. They wired their partisans throughout the state, warning that the close result might encourage attempts to steal the victory, as had occurred in the South eight years before. William C. Whitney volunteered to raise an additional $50,000 after election day to finance Democratic vigilance efforts. Simultaneously, Cleveland announced his conviction that he had been elected and his intention of making sure that no one cheated him out of his prize. In addition, Gorman called together a committee of fifty prominent lawyers to scrutinize and verify the results at a statewide level. In each of the New York counties, most of which Republicans controlled, he drafted five lawyers into similar service. Carl Schurz and Roscoe Conkling were just two of those who contributed their time and talents to making sure that Blaine would not prevail.

Actually, New York laws made any radical change in the official results announced on election night unlikely. If representatives of both parties had been present during the count, there could legally be no fraudulent ballots; each party's observers would presumably have prevented any irregularities perpetrated by the opposition. Therefore, no outside authority could question the announced returns unless someone could prove that a poll watcher had been bribed or intimidated. A recount would be impossible in any case, for all ballots were destroyed after being tallied and reported. A state canvassing board subsequently checked for clerical errors in the summation of local results or the inadvertent omission of some districts from the final tally. The board operated for a couple of weeks after the election, but it made only minor changes in the totals almost everyone had already accepted as giving Cleveland the Presidency.

The most conspicuous holdouts were Whitelaw Reid and his *Tribune*. Blaine did not quickly concede, and if the *Tribune* had its way, he never would have to do so. Even after Gould capitulated, Reid stubbornly refused to make a similar gesture, insisting that he would await the board of canvassers' report. He apparently hoped that massive Democratic frauds would come to light, although the board, as indicated, could hardly have done much anyway. The *Tribune's* pig-headedness in the face of virtually universal acceptance of the result was an outstanding example of partisan blindness. The Mugwump papers thoroughly enjoyed berating Reid's stand. They condemned the *Tribune* for faulty and deceitful reporting, contending that honest newspaper coverage would do much to improve the parties. The Mugwump press decided that the *Tribune* fell far short of its own standards, conveniently overlooking the distortions and oversimplifications it had perpetrated during the previous months.

Reid finally hauled down his victory banner on November 16, by which time the canvassing board had reaffirmed Cleveland's victory. Nationally, Cleveland had put together a slim plurality of popular votes. He fell short of an absolute majority because third-party candidates had attracted more than 300,000 votes. Cleveland's plurality amounted to less than 1 per cent of the almost ten million votes cast. Because of the regional distribution of his votes, however, Cleveland received a comfortable electoral margin of 219 to Blaine's 182—thanks to New York's 36 electoral votes, which Cleveland won with an officially recorded plurality of 1,149 votes out of almost 1.2 million cast, slightly less than .1 per cent of the state's votes. Cleveland thus became President with one of the narrowest victories the United States has ever seen.

The final margin was so small that Cleveland had obviously failed to receive a mandate from the people. With both platforms virtually interchangeable, no one could be voting for a particular set of programs. Instead, the result hung almost exclusively on party loyalty, efficient machines, and the candidates' personalities. The major party organizations had become so effective that each could call up an enormous number of votes without presenting any substantive political program. Yet, despite the Tweedledum and Tweedledee aspect of the parties and their failure to propose any startling new policies, some ten million enthusiastic and concerned voters had gone to the polls. Politics had truly become an end in itself.

Of course, the Mugwumps viewed the recently concluded campaign in a much different light. They felt that they had challenged the Republican party and scored a marvelous victory. If only 600 New York voters had cast ballots the other way, Blaine would be President. The New York Mugwump organizations knew that they had enlisted thousands of sympathizers, so they considered their impact profound and significant. Of course, every element that had worked for Cleveland in New York could make a similar claim. Ironically, had he won by a large margin, the responsibility of each of the groups that helped would have been correspondingly lessened, since Cleveland would, in that case, have won even without its assistance. The closeness of the result meant that every factor had been crucially necessary. Some historians have disparaged the Mugwumps' impact, listing a variety of other factors, including the Burchard incident that influenced the outcome. Certainly the 25,000 votes that Prohibition candidate St. John attracted critically reduced Blaine's New York totals. All that may be true, but it does not alter the fact that every Mugwump vote was vitally important. If the Independents had not revolted, Cleveland would not have won. The fact that a similar statement can be made for many other elements in no way diminishes the importance of the Mugwump interference with normal Republican party operations.

Throughout the campaign, the regular Republicans dismissed the Mugwumps as a negligible squad of malcontents, while the Independent rebels insisted that many thousands sympathized with them. Perhaps the most honest assessment of the size of the Independent Republican movement appeared in May, early in the race, when the *Nation* reported: "Nobody knows how large the Independent vote of this State is. In 1882 it developed enormous strength. . . . It may be that they only number 20,000, or that they number 200,000, but it makes no difference which. The important thing to know is that they number *enough* to give the state to whatever party they please." This struck the essential point: they did, after all, cast enough votes to ensure Cleveland's election and thus to defeat their enemy in the Republican party, James G. Blaine.

One area in which the Mugwumps had been extremely successful was in demonstrating the power of the press. Partisan newspapers had abounded prior to the campaign of 1884, but the journals that followed their editors and publishers out of the Republican party that year helped to create a powerful new force. Although the papers had to depend upon their own sales during the campaign, receiving no special contributions or favors from either party, the Mugwump message did not lack proponents. When a combined circulation of a half million or more issues was broadcasting their views in New York City alone, the Mugwumps knew their ideas reached many voters. The reactions of both the Republican and Democratic journals emphasized the point that Mugwump propaganda was proving influential. Partisan papers devoted a good bit of attention to damning or praising the Mugwump activities. The Independents' use of morality as an issue—a novel concept in political journalism—made the party press seem petty and malicious.

Immediately after the election, on November 6, the *New York Times* listed the Mugwumps' goals and ticked off their successes. Their first endeavor had been to force their own party to nominate a candidate they could support. To that end, they had spent several months creating an image of Blaine as a political jobber, totally unsuitable as a leader for the great Republican party. Over the previous eight years, they had rehearsed their campaign against the Plumed Knight and had developed strident arguments to discredit him. Working within the Republican party framework, they had sent delegates to Chicago and promoted an alternative candidate. They hoped against hope that the party would heed their cries, for they did not wish to leave it at that point. When the party totally ignored them, the Independents felt that the organization had proved undeserving of their further support.

The second great Mugwump goal, according to the *Times* survey, was to convince the Democrats to do what the Republicans had not done. Instead of committing themselves to a particular man, a course that had failed at the Republican convention, the Mugwumps maintained a more flexible attitude, indicating they would be happy with Cleveland should the Democrats choose to nominate him, but withholding their support until the Democratic convention had ended. When that convention's platform and nominee proved suitable, the rebelling Independent Republicans offered their fullest assistance to the Democratic Presidential effort. The Mugwumps took a good deal of credit for having influenced the Democratic party in favor of Cleveland, but, like many of their statements, this represented a good deal of wishful thinking. The Democrats would hardly have nominated anyone else regardless of what the Independent Republicans did.

Finally, the *Times* noted, the Mugwumps had endeavored "to arouse the conscience of the American people and break the long and weary slavery of sheer partisanship that has cursed the land and obtain an intelligent attention for the real interests involved in the administration of the Federal Government." The editorial concluded that the Mugwumps' entire program had accomplished this goal. A less biased commentator might question just how virtuous the movement's methods had been and how effectively they had stimulated popular concern about machine politics. In their fervent promotion of Cleveland, the Mugwumps had employed a good many of the partisan devices they so deplored. They had formed exclusive organizations, published inflammatory pamphlets, sent out rabble-rousing speakers, and slanted their news reporting. But although their methods were often partisan, their motives were not. The Independent Republicans never stooped to purchase or intimidate voters, and they stood to gain nothing more than personal satisfaction if their man won.

If one cannot fault the Mugwumps on motives, one can certainly question their ultimate success. There is no indication that they converted many Americans to the cause of good government. After the Mugwumps bolted, they formed organizations to reassure themselves of the correctness of their actions. Yet these same organizations insulated them from learning what the bulk of the Republican partisans were thinking and doing. The Mugwumps cautiously cooperated with the Democrats but remained scrupulously distinct from them, so they never really understood or influenced their allies either. This insulation and isolation from the mass of politically active men in the United States warped the Mugwumps' assessments of the results of their rebellion. Besides, only future developments would prove or disprove their contention that they had exerted a significant and beneficial influence upon United States politics and government.

One clearly unfortunate result of the Mugwump revolt was that it had divided and therefore weakened the reform movement. The schism between the Mugwumps and the Independent Republicans who refused to bolt in 1884 grew into an enormous gulf, making future cooperation strained or impossible. The Independents who remained loyal to the party profited from its vitality and influenced its choice of policies, but the revolt weakened their bargaining position, for they had demonstrated that they would stick with the party no matter what it did. Their party loyalty had proved stronger than their commitment to reform, and the party leaders therefore felt no need to change. As for the Mugwumps who had left the party, their attitudes mattered no more nor less than those of any other voters who chose not to support the regular Republican candidates. The reform movement had indeed suffered a debilitating division in 1884. Future reforms might come about, but not necessarily because of motivations and impulses similar to those the Mugwumps favored.

A large share of the blame for these disappointing consequences rests with the myopic Mugwumps who confused the noise they themselves were making with a national interest in cleaner politics. They narrowly focused their attention upon defeating the Republican candidate, and the anti-Blaine campaign gradually assumed such importance to them that it eclipsed all other considerations. The Mugwumps convinced themselves that Blaine as President would emasculate the Pendleton Act and reverse the trend toward reform. Therefore, defeating him became an end in itself, diverting their attention from their original goal of rescuing the nation from entrapment by an unresponsive party system.

In the final analysis, the Mugwumps themselves may have been the only ones interested at that time in changing the prevailing situation. In the days following the election, they thought a great deal about how they should proceed. The divergent motivations that had influenced various men to become Mugwumps made any unified postelection activity unlikely. The *New York Times* proposed that they maintain their associations and act as a sort of conscience for the Cleveland administration. As they claimed to have shared in electing the man, the Mugwumps considered it reasonable to assume that he would listen to their advice upon occasion. Having acted as a buffer between the parties, the Mugwumps could remain in that position, continuing to threaten and cajole party leaders into actions that would further their cause. But the *Times* suggestion could work only if the current party situation persisted. As long as the party labels did not represent differing philosophical viewpoints, a group of men dedicated to nonpartisan programs could readily switch their support from one party to the other depending upon which one showed the greater willingness to implement their programs. As the century drew to a close, however, issues did arise limiting the flexibility of independent voters.

For a brief period after the 1884 contest, however, an uncommitted stance remained feasible. Those who decided to remain suspended between the parties had to belong to the nonprofessional political class. They almost had to have private sources of income and no intention of using elective or appointive office to provide them with financial security. For this and other reasons, not all the rebels chose to remain in limbo between the parties. No political activist could stay outside the major party organizations, within which the only chances for advancement existed. As the Mugwumps' Cleveland clubs shut down after their victory celebrations, many of the bolters rejoined the Republican party. Throughout the campaign, they had protested their loyalty to the basic traditions of the party, although they felt antagonistic toward its current leadership. They could re-enter the party without hesitation once the voters had repudiated that leadership. A few went the opposite way and joined the Democratic party as full-fledged members. The remaining Mugwumps tried to play the role of political gadflies, but neither party paid much attention to them. As time went on, party planners simply wrote them off as unreliable and generally ignored their petulant protests and suggestions.

All this does not negate the basic achievements of the 1884

Mugwumps who broke their party ties to support the election of a new political leadership for the nation. No government created out of the existing political elements could ever have done all the Mugwumps wanted. Although they had won a tactical victory, their ultimate objective might well prove unattainable. Their exaggerated conception of their own importance and influence blinded them to the fact that Cleveland would inevitably be a Democrat. He might have fewer ties with corrupt members of his party than Blaine had with his corresponding associates, but Cleveland, nonetheless, remained beholden to that aggregation of contradictory and selfish interests that had nominated him. The Mugwumps had given him their support and their votes expecting no personal rewards, but most of the Democratic party exhibited no such philanthropic attitude. The Mugwumps praised Cleveland for his unknown qualities, but he stood upon the platform of a well-known party. At his very best, Cleveland could never have satisfied all the emotional aspirations of the self-righteous Mugwumps. In fact, they were fortunate that the succeeding years turned out as well as they did.

10. The Aftermath
of the Election

It seems too good to be true that, having got all the rascality and clap-trap of politics together in one heap, we have really swept it out of existence. Since the fall of Richmond there has been no such triumph in this country.

—*The Nation*, November 13, 1884

The difficulties facing the man in whom the Mugwumps had placed so much faith became obvious even before Cleveland took office. The reformers closely watched the President-elect's actions and were alarmed when he remained noncommittal on the civil-service question. Cleveland had said scarcely anything about his attitudes during the campaign, but the Mugwumps considered his continued silence afterwards extremely ominous. After the leading reformers had exchanged increasingly anxious correspondence, Cleveland finally responded to the National Independent Committee's entreaty for some statement on reform. His comments proved little more enlightening than had his letter to Curtis before the election, but at that, the Mugwumps might have done worse. They could scarcely have expected Cleveland to tie his hands on the matter of Presidential appointments when he was engaged in searching for qualified men for his cabinet, a difficult enough task in any case. He would only have compounded his problems by making blanket promises to the reformers.

Cabinet-making generally reveals the tenor and outlook of a President's administration, and Cleveland's choices were predictable. He overlooked the Mugwumps entirely, although some of them might well have proved superior to the partisans he chose. Cleveland made Bayard secretary of state, not because he had any diplomatic experience, but simply because he had been the other leading Democratic contender for the Presidency. By selecting Manning to be secretary of the treasury, Cleveland rewarded the manager who had done so much for him. The leading financier of his campaign, Whitney, had obviously earned his spot as head of the Navy Department. The relatively obscure partisans Cleveland placed in subordinate positions were known primarily at local levels, where the true strength of the Democratic party lay.

As unexciting in the White House as he had been in New York's executive mansion, Cleveland did little to surprise or frighten his Independent supporters. He permitted the reformed civil-service system to continue as it had been under Arthur. As Cleveland's administration wore on, the Mugwumps hoped he would concern himself with broadening the reach of the merit system. It would require no additional legislation for him to do so, for the Pendleton Act had granted the President sole authority to extend the reform. Cleveland eventually enlarged the system slightly to include more offices. By the end of his first four-year term, he had extended the Pendleton rules on tenure to encompass a larger percentage of federal officers. In the interim, of course, he had filled those offices with Democrats, thus guaranteeing his partisan backing while simultaneously seeking approval from the reformers. Some Mugwumps decried this action, but they should have expected it; the President naturally waited to expand the merit system until after he had rewarded his Democratic followers.

The reform issue lost much of its prominence, however, when Cleveland finally took an unequivocal position on tariff rates. He devoted his entire State of the Union address in December, 1887, to the tariffs, concluding that the protective duties were unreasonably high and calling for substantial reductions. The message and the inconclusive debates it stimulated in Congress during the spring of 1888 ensured that the tariff issue would have top priority in the upcoming Presidential race.

With a zest they had not exhibited since Blaine's defeat, the Republicans began their campaign early. The Democratic House remained divided over the tariff issue, and Republicans controlled the Senate, so the protectionists were able to head off any changes in the spring. At the Republican convention, the loyal Independent Republicans played a minor role. Blaine had refused to consider renomination, so the party chose an Indiana politician named Benjamin Harrison. Two considerations offset Harrison's unexceptional political record: he came from a doubtful state, and he was a grandson of former President William Henry Harrison. Fortunately, Republican campaigners could play down their candidate's weaknesses by concentrating on the tariff issue Cleveland had generously revived for them. They had modified and strengthened their machines after the near miss four years earlier, and they intended to make no mistakes this time.

Maintaining a firm hold on the patronage and possessing a record that had alienated few in his own party, the Democratic incumbent easily won renomination. Nevertheless, Cleveland's party had split over the tariff question, so Democratic spokesmen proved less effective than the unified Republicans. The reformers attracted little attention this time. Those Mugwumps who had not returned to the Republican party after the 1884 election campaigned tepidly for Cleveland or watched from the sidelines. Loyal Independent Republicans felt no particular animus toward Harrison, who seemed no worse, if no better, than Hayes or Garfield had been. Civil-service reform caused little comment although both parties remained officially committed to it through their platforms. Cleveland had not opposed broadening the merit system, and most assumed that Harrison would do the same.

The election came to an unsatisfying conclusion. The Democrats lost Indiana, as expected, and New York as well in a
Republican sweep of the electoral college, 233 to 168. Having
also captured control of both houses of Congress, the Grand
Old Party began acting like the majority party once again.
This naturally angered the Democrats, who had managed to
run up a popular plurality of 100,000 votes for Cleveland. Party
machines on both sides had worked overtime to produce a full
voter turnout. In the process, the South fell further under
Democratic influence, ensuring Cleveland even larger majorities
than in 1884. Meanwhile, the Republicans had concentrated their
attention on the doubtful states. The changeover in Congress
fully justified the Republicans' cocky attitudes. When Harrison
installed Blaine as secretary of state, the party appeared to have
fully vindicated itself. Controlling both legislative and executive
branches for the first time since 1882, the Republicans over-
played their hand.

The Fifty-First Congress eventually earned a disparaging nickname, The Billion Dollar Congress, in recognition of its huge
appropriations bills. As a slap at the Democrats, the Republicans
pushed through the McKinley Tariff in 1890, which established
the highest protective rates ever set up to that point. They also
responded to business and popular pressure by approving the
Sherman Antitrust Act. This gesture proved empty in the next
few years, for both Republican and Democratic Presidents failed
to implement it. Finally, the Republicans revised the old Bland-
Allison Silver Purchase Act of 1878. Passed over heavy opposition from the silver interests, the 1890 Sherman Silver Purchase
Act empowered the treasury to buy and coin four million ounces
of silver at the current market price, rather than at the artificially
high legal ratio of sixteen to one. This program satisfied neither
gold-standard advocates nor those who favored free silver, but
as a compromise measure, it worked fairly well.

These legislative actions failed to impress the people, and the
off-year elections of 1890 did not go well for the Republicans.
They lost control of the House and began to fear another Democratic take-over. Only at this point did Harrison respond to the
civil-service-reform impulse. Acting as a typical spoilsman, he
had originally swept the Democrats in unprotected positions out

of office, but, to the Mugwumps' relief, he had then appointed Theodore Roosevelt commissioner of the civil service. Roosevelt's strong reform convictions may have helped prevent a reduction in the number of offices under merit rules, but until a Democratic victory seemed imminent, no expansion took place. Copying Cleveland, at the end of his term Harrison extended the tenure provisions to additional members of the civil service. In this way he locked in many of his own partisans, just as Cleveland had protected Democrats in 1888. The reformers were hardly impressed with Harrison's patently partisan gesture, but at least no reduction had occurred. Once a particular position fell under the merit system, a President was very reluctant to remove it. In spurts, then, a professional bureaucracy gradually increased its influence.

While the Republican government in Washington had busied itself providing more tariff protection for America's infant industries, a rural rebellion had broken out. In both the Republican Midwest and the Democratic South, agrarian elements had become increasingly discontented, and the major parties did not seem concerned with their particular needs. One of the major goals of the Mugwump rebellion had been to shock the parties into realizing that they should serve the interests of the people. The rural revolt was a logical consequence of their failure to do so. The farmers did what the Mugwumps had not: they began their protests at local levels. The Patrons of Husbandry had originated as a social outlet for farmers, but these Grangers had soon organized into special-interest groups able to push the so-called Granger Laws through state legislatures. Since the prevailing method of determining political divisions often discriminated in favor of rural residents, the farmers could exert a disproportionate influence in getting state authorities to regulate grain elevators, railroads, and other enterprises that seemed to be siphoning off their profits. Local politicians recognized the importance of the agrarian protests and encouraged the major parties to respond. In the agricultural heartland of the nation, this newly awakened political force grew and prospered.

In 1886, the Supreme Court discouraged the state regulatory movements by denying the constitutionality of an Illinois law setting rates for an interstate railroad. The Constitution explicitly allocates to Congress the authority to regulate interstate commerce. Thwarted at the state level, the farm protesters turned their attention to Washington. The very next year, Congress responded with an act creating the Interstate Commerce Commission to regulate railroad operations much as state laws had done. Actually, railroad entrepreneurs caught in debilitating competition had lobbied energetically for just such a commission, but the rural rebels cheered it as their own success. Although subsequent court decisions and legislative changes rendered the commission almost powerless, its very creation whetted farmers' demands for a more responsive government nationwide.

In many ways, the farmers resembled the civil-service reformers. Both groups wanted a government that would listen to and act on their complaints. Both objected to the neglect they suffered when special interests and machines dominated the government. And, as the Mugwumps had concluded in 1884, organization seemed to offer the most effective way of attracting attention. Where the Mugwumps had been able to create only a small, if vocal, protest association, the farmers represented a large and enterprising group. Furthermore, they had already succeeded in influencing state government, and they had developed sound local establishments before they attempted to affect national politics. Thus they started out in a much stronger position than the Mugwumps had in trying to get their demands translated into action. To make a major impression on the American political scene, they had simply to call together the multitude of local and regional organizations and meld them into a national coalition.

Fortunately, some huge regional groupings already existed. The formation of the Southern Alliance in Texas in 1875 stimulated the establishment of a Northern Alliance in 1880. In addition, the Colored Farmers' Alliance sprang up in the Southern states where white farmers refused to associate with black ones. By the end of the 1880's, these quasi-political farmers' organizations had enrolled millions of persons. Individual alliance members voted as they chose, but they became increasingly disenchanted with the major party attitudes toward rural grievances. The Harrison Administration's lack of interest in their proposals triggered a coalescing of alliance members into the People's or, more familiarly, the Populist party. A strong third-party organization had finally risen to challenge the two major ones. It had all the elements necessary to compete with its opponents, as it was founded upon a broad popular basis and possessed persuasive leaders and experienced organizers.

Ignored by the regular parties, the People's party held its first Presidential convention in July, 1892. Over the years, rural activists had developed a comprehensive set of programs, including government ownership of railroads, a graduated income tax, free coinage of silver, and a labor program to attract urban voters. Significantly, the Populist platform also suggested strengthening the average citizen's voice in politics through such proposals as the direct election of senators and the secret ballot. Finally, it included a strongly worded civil-service-reform plank. The Populist Presidential nominee, ex-Greenbacker General James B. Weaver, did surprisingly well, polling over a million popular votes in the election and winning some electoral ones as well, primarily in the West. The Populist ticket prospered there because it sponsored free silver, which neither of the major parties favored.

Meanwhile, the Republicans and the Democrats fought another round in their predictable partisan face-off, with incumbent Harrison now forced to defend his party's tariff, and the renominated Cleveland on the offensive. For the third time, Cleveland won a popular plurality. He managed to nail down a majority of 277 electoral votes to Harrison's 145 and Weaver's 22. The Democratic party also put together a majority in both House and Senate, giving it total federal control, something it had not enjoyed since before the Civil War. Vindicated and resolute, Cleveland took the helm and six months later found the ship of state wallowing in the worst depression it had suffered since the mid-1870's, possibly in its entire history. The economic problems major parties had neglected combined with the agricultural depression, which had already spurred the agrarian protests, facing Cleveland with his most difficult test.

The Democratic President struggled to solve the problems in accordance with his conservative philosophy. First, he had Congress revoke the Sherman Silver Purchase Act, insisting that the nation could thrive only on a gold standard. Then his partisans attacked the tariff, but the resulting Wilson-Gorman Bill satisfied no one, least of all the President, who despairingly permitted it to become law without his signature. The over-all tariff levels dropped some, but the revised rates merely created new injustices. As the depression worsened, Cleveland found himself a target for criticism on all sides. The nation's emotional climax came in 1894, when the Pullman Strike paralyzed the railroad system. Meanwhile, Cleveland fought his own party over the money question. He forced four separate gold-bonding bills through a reluctant Congress in order to maintain the U.S. Treasury's solvency in the metal. Nothing the President did, however, relieved the nation's economic distress.

In 1894, Cleveland's congressional margin disappeared, leaving him virtually helpless in the White House. The Populists put on a stunning performance, while Republican successes encouraged the party's leaders to think they had the 1896 Presidential race won. All they had to do was stand aside and watch the Democratic party commit suicide. Irreconcilable differences within the Democratic coalition limited its ability to rule in a time of crisis. Democratic protectionists and low-tariff men had long since despaired of reaching any agreement; now bickering between Gold Bugs and free-silver advocates made the party incapable of action. Contradictions within the party between the elements associated with Cleveland's conservative backers and those who represented labor and farm voters grew more serious by the hour. Ironically, a revived and restructured Republican party stood ready to snatch the power the divided Democrats seemed hopelessly unable to handle.

The renewed strength the Republican party displayed in the late 1890's stemmed in part from a realization that civil-service reform would ultimately succeed. President Cleveland had retained Theodore Roosevelt in his post at the Civil Service Commission until the Independent Republican decided to resign in 1895. Cleveland did a good deal to expand the scope of the merit system during his second term, and his successor, McKinley, would do little to reverse the trend. In absolute numbers, however, more civil servants remained outside the rules than had been excluded under the first authorizations of the Pendleton Act. This circumstance developed because of a tremendous increase in the total number of federal civil servants in the last two decades of the nineteenth century. In 1900, of more than 200,000 total federal employees, only about 95,000 fell under civil-service rules. Many of the rest were postal employees in smaller districts, where merit rules would have been difficult to implement in any case. Those left outside the system represented little more than a remnant of the former spoils system, however, for the parties had lost control over the selection of civil servants in the more responsible, powerful positions. When Theodore Roosevelt, a confirmed reformer in this area, became President, he placed the vast majority of civil servants under merit rules.

Despite an over-all increase in the number of men serving in federal offices, the practice of fund-raising by assessing their salaries had decreased sharply. Those in protected positions made voluntary contributions less frequently, and partisans who felt an obligation to the party contributed in or out of office. To that extent, at least, civil-service reform had succeeded in helping to insulate the bureaucracy from the parties. Whether this always resulted in better government is less clear. The nonpartisan selection process put more qualified men in government offices, but the merit system also guaranteed tenure. Job security may have been as conducive to unimaginative administration as party loyalty had been to inefficiency in the old days. At best, the party no longer had so many hangers-on collecting federal salaries to do party business. Generally, the reformers could view the civil-service system with some satisfaction.

The reformers' concomitant goal—weakening the influence of machines and party leaders—was not fulfilled. The Mugwumps had gravely underestimated the vitality of party organizations. The Independents had acted on the premise that the machines depended primarily upon spoils. Politicians certainly did exploit spoils as long as they were available, but in no sense did the machines entirely depend upon patronage rewards. As the merit system gradually reduced the usefulness of the patronage, the bosses increasingly relied upon other sources of income and influence, generally behind the scenes. In a sense, this made them even more of a threat to the people's welfare. As partisan operations became less conspicuous, it became more difficult to arouse public sentiment against the bosses.

The methods these political leaders began to emphasize were not new, but they did represent refinements of earlier machine operations. Thomas Collier Platt stands as a prime example of the new breed of bosses. He had risen to prominence in the Conkling machine and had early learned to appreciate the benefits of machines. He had also seen Conkling mercilessly destroyed in his battle with Hayes and Garfield over patronage. Having lost his Senate seat along with the boss in 1881, Platt did not drop out of politics. Instead, he worked steadily to rehabilitate the New York Republican party. By the 1890's, out of the remnants of the old machine, he had constructed the ideal of the new. He obviously could not count upon income from the New York Customhouse, which had fallen under the Pendleton Act's original jurisdiction, and he had lost other lucrative spoils as well. The remainder consisted of smaller federal dependencies which the Pendleton rules had not covered and which also provided substantially fewer profits. The revived Platt machine thrived instead upon the significant participation of corporations in politics.

State bosses had always exercised some influence over corporations, which depended upon local chartering regulations. The strike bills of the 1870's had gradually given way to a systematic and less wasteful procedure in the 1890's. Platt acted as something of an ombudsman for wealthy interests in his state. When an industrialist wanted the legislature to alter his charter or state authorities to condone a questionable deal, he would contact the New York boss. Platt then instructed his subordinates in the state legislature or in the courts to do the industrialist's bidding. In return, the grateful manufacturer would contribute generously to the party's campaign chest. With the money thus generated, Platt's machine could influence the course of future elections and perpetuate itself in power. The arrangement proved agreeable for all concerned. Platt kept his machine healthy and powerful; favor seekers got their wishes fulfilled at a reasonable cost. They no longer needed to bribe several individuals; one big contribution would take care of the whole problem.

Previously, the struggle for offices, the demands for contributions from officeholders, and the exorbitant bribery of elected representatives had been wasteful, time consuming, and dangerous. Under the revised system, the boss need never take a prominent or exposed position. He thus escaped the criticism Tweed or Conkling suffered, for he was doing nothing obviously illegal. Contributions to the parties were considered not only acceptable but necessary for their survival. Any individual had the freedom to contribute his money to whatever political organization he chose. The legislative actions the machines helped to promote were no more than could be expected in a nation where special-interest groups had traditionally gained a hearing. The general public might suffer in the long run, but until the people managed to organize themselves into a more powerful interest group, they had no effective way of complaining.

As the 1896 Presidential election loomed, the Republican organizations methodically went into operation. Never so internally disoriented as the Democratic party, the Republican coalition felt that it knew how to solve the economic problems plaguing the nation. Obviously, Republican spokesmen claimed, it was Democratic tampering with the tariffs that had caused the economic disaster. The Grand Old Party had an ideal candidate to reverse that trend in the person of William McKinley. The Ohio politician's name was associated with the heavily protective tariff that the Fifty-First Congress had promulgated six years earlier, and he appeared to be sound on all other issues as well. The astute machinations of his friend and adviser, Marcus Alonzo Hanna, assured McKinley the nomination. In fact, the 1896 Republican convention's only controversy concerned the money question. McKinley himself did not oppose bimetallism, a dependence upon both gold and silver as basic monetary standards. The party leaders overruled him, coming out solidly for the undiluted gold standard. A disgruntled contingent of silver Republicans walked out of the convention, but McKinley's campaign rested in safe hands. As the nominee's political mentor, Mark Hanna masterminded the Republican party at the national level. Hanna had retired young from business to devote himself to politics and became a wizard at political managing and maneuvering. Once he had decided to boost William McKinley to the Presidency, he permitted no obstacles to impede him. He came about as close to being a national party boss as the United States has ever had. Exploiting the solid, conservative image that Platt and others like him had built for the party at local levels, Hanna made the national Republican party quite attractive to the business community. The gold standard and high protective tariffs served as the principal features of the 1896 Republican party's image, and Hanna used them to woo bankers and manufacturers to his camp. Rather than wait for contributions to materialize, Hanna simply told banks, industrialists, and merchants how much their fair share would be. He might tap a Rockefeller for $250,000 or a bank for a percentage of its total assets. Using sure and smooth techniques, Hanna collected a fantastic campaign fund for his man, estimated at from ten million to sixteen million dollars. The Democratic party had to operate its entire 1896 Presidential canvass on something less than a half million dollars. The Democrats would never again come near to matching the Republican party's financial backing, as it had done in the 1880's.

In fact, by 1896, the Democratic party had all but disintegrated. Those reformers who had been hoping for just such a collapse for years were probably none too happy with the reality. The party was not falling apart because of poor government or the death of the spoils system, but because a reviving interest in pressing issues made its old alignments unworkable. The Democratic party had always consisted of a more or less fragile coalition of elements; now some of these began to spin off. Democratic partisans had never found cooperation easy, and, in 1894 and 1895, the unifying hatred of Republicanism came second to factionalism within the party. Resembling the Half-Breed–Stalwart struggles of the Republican party when it had been in power, these factional divisions in the Democratic party appeared to have mortally wounded it. Whether or not the party could continue as a viable organization became debatable in the dark days of the mid-1890's. Through it all, that rock of imperturbability, Grover Cleveland, remained heedless to popular outcry and apparently unconcerned over the impact his actions might have on the party's future. He considered his actions correct and allowed nothing to turn him aside.

The Populists watched and waited. They fully expected the Democrats under Cleveland's leadership to espouse the gold standard the Republican party had already announced as its own. Then the Populists could make a virtue out of necessity by emphasizing free silver. Unfortunately, like the Mugwumps' narrow concentration on patronage in 1884, the Populists' dependence upon a single issue spelled disaster. They had won most of their electoral votes in 1892 for their silver stand, so they neglected the broad list of proposals they had drafted four years earlier. Their chance to sweep into a position of equality with the major parties hinged on the Democrats' acting in favor of gold.

Delegates to the 1896 Democratic convention were hopelessly split over both the tariff and money issues. The party's silverites had planned ahead by creating publicity organizations and pressure groups. Mining executives also guaranteed them financial support, something that most of the others in the assembly lacked. In opposition stood Cleveland's friends, with the backing of the party's business interests. The gold-standard men had maintained an appearance of strength behind the man in the White House, but it proved illusory as the silver men wooed convention delegates. The President controlled the remaining patronage, but he refused to manipulate it, having decided against running for a fourth time. To no one's surprise, platform considerations set the stage for a decision on the nominee. When the resolutions committee failed to agree, it threw the money question open on the convention floor. Three men spoke in favor of a free-silver plank, but one thoroughly entranced the delegates. The enthusiastic reception of William Jennings Bryan's Cross of Gold speech signaled the end of conservative control in the Democratic party and the emergence of a new image.

The convention forthwith adopted not only free silver but Bryan as well. In the turmoil that followed, a good many gold advocates walked out, just as the silverites had left the Republican convention some weeks before.

Like the Mugwumps a decade earlier, the leaders of the People's party had underestimated the inherent strengths of the established parties. Populists had all but forgotten their comprehensive platform as they became fixated on the free-silver plank. In shifting its position, the Democratic coalition completely outflanked the agrarian agitators. Both major parties were so broadly based that some members of each favored free silver. In addition, the Democrats recognized the political bankruptcy of the incumbent President's philosophy. So, with few backward glances, the Democratic party moved over and engulfed the single principle upon which the Populists had gambled all.

Meeting shortly after the Democratic convention had stolen their chief issue, the Populists lamely nominated Bryan, although they insisted on putting up a candidate of their own for the Vice-Presidency. The agrarians had little choice, for Bryan represented almost everything the rural coalition stood for. He had made himself famous in Nebraska by defending Populist ideals from a Democratic platform. The Populist convention could never have found so talented a spokesman in its own membership, and so it made the decision that effectively destroyed the party's individuality. The two-party system thus survived its most serious challenge since the Civil War.

For the frenetic Presidential canvass of 1896, both major parties dressed themselves in new or restyled clothing. The Republican party had fostered its reputation as the sound-money, sound-economic-policy party in the country. The trend toward big-business support of the Republican party would become a semipermanent aspect of the political picture. Meanwhile, Democratic economic policies had proved disastrous. The Democrats simply could no longer offer industrialists and railroad men the promise of stability as the party under Cleveland had done. When the Gold Bugs lost to Bryan, the Democratic party lost its appeal to its more conservative backers, who fled to the safer haven the Republicans provided. Having made the jump, they discovered the benefits available from smoothly efficient Republican machines. Thus, the money issue came to symbolize a new polarization of the parties.

The farmers and the "little" men sided with the Democrats. The Populist party had arisen because farmers felt ignored in national policies. The Republican party seemed to care very little about them, but the Democrats sounded like Populists when Bryan spoke for them. For years, the Democratic party had worked to attract labor, and, inasmuch as free silver represented cheap money, this attraction increased. Consequently, at the same time as the Republican party was enticing and reinforcing business support, the Democratic party seemed bent on serving the wage earner and the farmer. The image the Democratic party adopted in this campaign persisted in the years to come. After all, as Bryan himself ran for the Presidency again in 1900 and 1908, the party could hardly shake off his rural attitudes. In 1896, the party platforms finally sounded different after twenty years of similarity. Party labels appeared to mean something at last.

A polarization of party attitudes could never be complete, nor could it happen overnight. Years of tradition lay behind. Had it occurred without such a history, the development of these generalized images would suggest that a Republican party of the rich but few would lose to a Democratic party of the poor but numerous. It did not work out that way. Party loyalty did not suddenly disappear; myriad factors prevented the sorting out of the disadvantaged on one side and the wealthy on the other. For example, farmers in the Midwest who had always voted Republican might have considered a Populist alternative, but they simply could not overcome years of habit; consequently, they voted against the party that had just attempted to assume a stance as an agrarian champion. Cleveland's antidepression policies convinced many who had no relationship whatever with the Republican industrial interests that a vote for his party would be foolish, even though the Democratic party had just repudiated Cleveland and reoriented itself at its convention. The new alignments tended to benefit Republican candidates more than they did Democratic ones.

The campaign of 1896 developed into one of the most exhausting in years. Bryan stumped the nation, speaking everywhere in favor of free silver. McKinley's managers had intended to make criticism of the Wilson-Gorman Tariff the primary issue, but Bryan's attack forced tariff considerations to the rear. McKinley remained at his home in Canton, Ohio, during most of the campaign, while trainloads of well-wishers flowed into and out of the town to hear him speak from his porch. Campaigners from both parties debated the money issue to death, but Bryan's oratorical skill held the crowds, who listened spellbound. On election day, inevitably, he came up wanting. McKinley swept in with an impressive plurality of over a half million votes out of about fourteen million cast. Faced with meaningful political alternatives for the first time since Reconstruction, the American people chose to tie their hopes to the Republican party, which had done a thorough job of restructuring itself in the past few years. The new Republican party might not have been exactly what the reformers had hoped to create, but it proved popular.

The McKinley-Bryan race signaled the end of the conditions that had fostered the civil-service-reform movement of the 1870's and 1880's. The Independent Republicans had justified their revolt in 1884 by maintaining, quite correctly, that the two parties were identical in outlook and philosophy. Therefore, a conscientious voter could choose between candidates for personal reasons rather than on the basis of party designations. This was no longer true. By 1896, the two parties had become so obviously differentiated on major issues that Mugwump behavior seemed unrealistic. A voter's attitude toward the tariff or money question effectively determined which party's candidate he would support.

Furthermore, in the years following the 1884 contest, the Mugwumps had observed that their efforts had brought about few fundamental changes. In pursuing their goals they had followed an increasingly narrow path, first concentrating their full attention upon civil-service reform and then devoting all their energy to the election of a single man. To achieve the latter result, they had sacrificed what influence they possessed within the Republican party. This limiting and focusing of their attention had also destroyed their flexibility, and the Mugwumps became virtually incapable of furthering their goals. The Republican party machines not only survived the loss of their patronage and the defeat of Blaine but revived stronger still; the Mugwumps had already expended all of the ammunition in their arsenal and were no longer an integral element in party affairs. The reformers' devotion to ultimately ineffective means made the achievement of their ends impossible.

A major weakness in the Mugwumps' campaign had involved their own narrowness. They staked everything on a merit system, but a reformed civil service alone simply could not destroy the machines. Bosses could thrive with or without federal patronage, and the proof of that statement lay right under the Mugwumps' noses in New York City. While they zealously attacked the federal and state spoils systems, hoping to choke off the bosses' sustenance, Democratic machines continued to organize, control, and plunder all around them. The reformers had cut off one of the party organization's sources of power only to have others, even less responsive to the popular will, spring up in its place. Political jobbery for the benefit of special-interest groups prevailed.

The Independent Republicans had erred fundamentally in assuming that an attack leveled at the national party structure would force it to reform. They were still thinking in terms of the sort of centralized party created by loyalty to a leader like Jackson, or by strong positions on the slavery issue, the war, and Radical Reconstruction. As interest in these last issues, which crossed state boundaries, declined in the 1870's, so, too, did the relative importance of the national Republican party. The Mugwump program was founded on the premise that the vital organs of the party lay at the federal level. In the 1880's and 1890's, this premise was invalid.

The Independent Republicans who stayed behind in the party, suffering criticism and vituperation from their rebelling fellows, probably accomplished much more in the long run. Although most of them remained loyal for personal reasons, their positions in the party enabled them to shape it more effectively than the Mugwumps could after 1884. Many of the nonrebelling Independents became leaders of the Progressive movement in the early 1900's. As members in good standing of a basically conservative party, the Progressive Republicans gradually developed a good deal of influence.

They enjoyed much more success than the Mugwumps had in getting action at all levels of government. The national Progressive movement, like the Populist one, had firm foundations at local levels. Some of the most effective Progressive leaders operated in large cities—for example, Tom Johnson in Cleveland, Samuel Jones in Toledo, and Hazen Pingree in Detroit. Gradually, the reform attitudes spread beyond city limits. The epitome of the state Progressive leader was Robert M. LaFollette of Wisconsin. By the 1880's he had worked his way up to a seat in the U.S. House of Representatives by voting along straight Republican party lines. Then his popularity waned until he won the state governorship in 1900 on a reform platform calling for primary elections, regulation of corporations, and the use of experts in government. He constructed a powerful machine for himself in Wisconsin and, like the bosses of the Gilded Age, had himself sent to the Senate, where he remained for twenty years. The major difference between LaFollette and other bosses lay in their philosophy and programs. LaFollette advocated political reform at all levels, as did Albert B. Cummins in Iowa and George W. Norris in Nebraska.

Under the benevolent Presidency of that old Independent Republican, Theodore Roosevelt, the Progressives became a powerful faction in the Republican party. They borrowed many proposals from past reform movements, including a strong commitment to the merit system. Progressives also revived some of the Populist methods for making government more responsive to the people and less dependent upon machines. The direct election of senators was incorporated in a constitutional amendment in 1913 as a result of their efforts. They encouraged the use of a primary election system to give the people the responsibility for making nominations rather than leaving such crucial decisions to party caucuses and conventions. They enfranchised women and, at the state level, instituted referendum, recall, and the initiative. Although the implementation of these reforms never proved as beneficial as the Progressives hoped, at least they had a variety of approaches to try, rather than only one, as the Mugwumps had.

Ironically, the Progressives' success stemmed from their capturing and altering the party organizations that the Mugwumps had so bitterly criticized. It was a case of fighting fire with fire. An energetic, disciplined Progressive organization could defeat a conservative or corrupt machine and use the power gained for its own purposes. A local Progressive machine gave the national leader a fallback position and a reliable source of support. So the Progressives proved to be much more flexible and long-lived than the Mugwumps. The Progressives had recognized that a national party's true vitality lay in its diversified local organizations. To fight the machines one had essentially to join them and remodel them from the inside. And the Progressives won their most significant victories while they maintained their ties with the regular parties, not by breaking them as the Mugwumps had in 1884. The early rebels were too hasty, too narrow, and too idealistic to consider the successful if expedient course their Progressive heirs would follow.

11. Conclusion

*Our political and governmental processes have grown so unresponsive,
so ill-designed for contemporary purposes, that they waste the tax-
payers' money, mangle good programs and smother every good man
who gets into the system.*

—JOHN W. GARDNER, Chairman, National
Urban Coalition, July, 1970

The major consequences of the civil-service-reform movement's
thirty-year run took some time to materialize. The merit system
that the Independent Republicans helped initiate and the Mugwumps fought to protect has grown and thrived in the twentieth
century. With the exception of the highest-level positions, professional bureaucrats handle all administrative functions, while
supposedly remaining apolitical. The Hatch Act of 1939 deline-
ated exactly how politically active civil servants may be. The
main measure of the extent of the reformers' influence is that a
merit system has become standard for administrators and
employees at all levels of civil service.

The reformers also hoped that their program would destroy
self-seeking party organizations and foster decent government.
The creation of a professional bureaucracy, however, has not

guaranteed wise administration of government, nor has it fundamentally altered the operations of the major parties. Machines
still exist, some of which differ little from those of the Gilded
Age. The decision to form the citizens' lobby group Common
Cause in 1970 indicates that an individual still has difficulty
making his wishes known at top government levels. Special-
interest groups, lobbyists, and those willing to contribute heavily
to political campaigns all have access to officials and influence
over political decisions denied the less aggressive or less wealthy
person. The Mugwumps' desire to foster more responsive government at every level appears far from fulfillment at present.

In recent years the increasing importance of national as compared to local issues has substantially altered the behavior of
politicians and parties. In part, this is a result of the expanded
role of the federal government in American society. The social-
welfare legislation New Deal congresses approved bypassed local
efforts, and the trend toward a national welfare state has continued ever since. The enormous efforts the national government
exerted during the two world wars greatly increased federal
influence, and that influence has hardly declined in the years
since. Developments in mass communication have brought to
the people awareness of national policies and programs. The
federated national parties still exist, but they derive much of
their authority from the federal level. The Mugwumps' approach
—tackling problems at the national level—would be much more
sensible today than it was in the 1880's.

The problem the Mugwumps faced—how best to alter the
existing system—troubles reformers today as well. The Mugwumps chose to abandon their party positions and try to influence the course of political events from outside the regular
organizations. In the long run, this tactic proved unsuccessful.
Those Independents who stayed with the Republican party were
the ones who ultimately helped determine what changes would
occur. An organized political party possesses strengths and
resiliencies developed over long years of operation, and it may
itself offer the most effective way of bringing about political
change. Many may decide, as did some Independents in 1884,
that the flaws in a party's leaders are too great to ignore. Those

who choose to work outside of the existing organizations, however, may well discover that their suggestions are not being
heeded.

Nevertheless, a notable legacy of those reformers who broke
their ties with the Republican party in 1884 concerns the
respectability of independent political behavior. Frequently during the campaign and after Cleveland's election, Mugwump
publicists stressed the importance of establishing a precedent
for conscientious political activity outside of the regular party
organizations. The Mugwumps considered themselves pioneers
in this direction, and they constantly encouraged others to
reassess their commitments to the regular parties. For a number
of reasons, independent voting behavior has become much more
common. These days, voters seem to care less whether a man
calls himself a Democrat or Republican and more whether he
subscribes to liberal or conservative principles. Party loyalty
persists, but it has suffered severe strains in recent years. A
party certainly cannot remain deaf to the people's desires or
ignorant of changing political realities.

The survival of the two major parties through crises and radi-
cally altered conditions since the Civil War indicates something
of the strength of these organizations. Indeed, some serious
drawbacks accompany the sort of political polarization that can
develop in the absence of broad-ranging parties. If a major party
takes a definite stand, as, for example, the Republican party did
under the leadership of conservative spokesman Barry Goldwater
in 1964, it can attract a substantial group of supporters. But it
will not necessarily attract enough votes to put itself into power.
The American electorate thus far has proved too diverse and
fickle to give majority support to a particular set of principles.
The dull, homogenized parties of the 1880's and 1890's fulfilled
a need that parties dedicated to specific ideals simply could not
meet. If every politician makes clear his stand to the Right or
Left, it may stimulate meaningful discussion of the issues, but
it will also make achievement of a consensus unlikely. A Congress consisting of representatives of a number of parties, each
unswervingly dedicated to a single objective, could seldom
function effectively.

In short, compromise is advisable. Then as now, the ambiguous party labels, which the Mugwumps criticized as concealing a multitude of evils, enabled men with a variety of conflicting views to cooperate. In the Gilded Age, a Stalwart could remain a Republican even though Half-Breeds might be in control. He could retreat or adapt, yet always retain his basic Republicanism unchallenged. A similar situation exists today. A nonprofessional who merely wishes to do his civic duty can make his decisions without difficulty on the basis of party labels. His faith in the worthiness of a party may well be misplaced, but it comforts him. Moral principles seldom apply in the day-to-day give and take of politics. The high-minded man who continues to work within his party, as did the nonbolting Independent Republicans, may have to swallow his principles now and then, but he may also be able to exercise a continuing beneficent influence through time.

Compromise and cooperation within the political parties of the nineteenth century helped teach politicians how to compromise and cooperate with members of the opposition party when necessary. Party rule as practiced obviously did not produce outstanding government. The Mugwumps failed to admit, however, that the type of governing that did take place probably satisfied the American people at the time. The strength that enabled the parties to weather the reform attack also ensured their continued capacity to operate despite adverse circumstances. In the long run, the reformers' efforts did help to limit, if not to eliminate, partisan corruption. They could not destroy the party structures that had developed. With all their defects and excesses, these organizations still symbolize the ability of a diversity of Americans to live together in some sort of working unity.

Bibliographic Essay

The research for this book included investigation of archival holdings of many individuals involved in the election of 1884, in particular the George William Curtis papers and the James Russell Lowell papers at the Houghton Library of Harvard University; the John Forester Andrew papers, the Edward A. Atkinson papers, and the John D. Long papers at the Massachusetts Historical Society; and the Silas W. Burt papers at the New-York Historical Society. The many newspapers published during the period are very useful primary sources. Not surprisingly, the *New York Times* appears to have been the most rational member of the Mugwump press, although the *New York Herald* maintained the largest circulation of any of the rebel papers. The *New York Evening Post* and the *Nation*, both under E. L. Godkin's control, added spice to the campaign. *Harper's Weekly* consistently argued in favor of idealistic action, while Thomas Nast's cartoons livened the journal's pages. Whitelaw Reid's anti-Mugwump campaign in the *New York Tribune* never failed to provide colorful reading. Joseph Pulitzer had just taken over the *New York World*, and he exploited campaign news to build his paper into a rival of the established giants. Meanwhile, ex-Democrat Charles Dana wrote some of the most acid editorials of all in his lonely campaign for Ben Butler in the *New York Sun*. In addition, the numerous pamphlets and speeches printed by the various Mugwump or Independent Republican organizations gave insights into rebel thinking.

The most recent general secondary work on the Gilded Age is H. Wayne Morgan's *From Hayes to McKinley* (1969), which focuses almost exclusively upon Presidential politics and thus neglects many significant local political developments. Robert H. Wiebe's *The Search for Order 1877–1920* (1967) sketches in broad detail the social, economic, and political impulses that buffeted the nation at the turn of the century. The classic study of the period is *The Politicos* (1938) by Matthew Josephson, which emphasizes the influence of businessmen on politics. The best multivolume history of the period is Ellis Paxson Oberholtzer's *A History of the United States since the Civil War,* 5 vols. (1931). On political matters, Edward Stanwood's *A History of the Presidency from 1788 to 1897* (1928) and Joseph Bucklin Bishop's *Presidential Nominations and Elections* (1916) are thorough and relatively unbiased. Harrison Cook Thomas published a sound study specifically on *The Return of the Democratic Party to Power in 1884* (1919).

Anyone studying late-nineteenth-century politics must familiarize himself with two outstanding contemporary studies: James Bryce's *The American Commonwealth* (1888) and Moisei Ostrogorski's *Democracy and the Organization of Political Parties, Vol. II: The United States* (1902). Both Englishman Bryce and Russian Ostrogorski made exhaustive comparative studies of British and American parties. Although E. E. Schattschneider's *Party Government* (1942) is not a history, its description of the American party system is valid for the Gilded Age. Three good recent books on elements of the political structure are Alexander B. Callow, Jr.'s *The Tweed Ring* (1965); David J. Rothman's *Politics and Power: The U.S. Senate, 1869–1901* (1966); and Robert D. Marcus's *Grand Old Party: Political Structure in the Gilded Age, 1880–96* (1971). The last confines its attention almost exclusively to the Republican national committees of the period, describing the decentralized national parties.

The chief political issues of the Gilded Age included sectionalism, tariffs, and civil-service reform. Stanley P. Hirshson's *Farewell to the Bloody Shirt* (1962) describes the declining attention Northern Republicans gave to the lot of Southern blacks after 1877. Edward Stanwood's *American Tariff Controversies in the Nineteenth Century,* 2 vols. (1903) and Frank W. Taussig's *The Tariff History of the United States* (1892), which eventually ran through eight editions, are both well done. Ari Hoogenboom's *Outlawing the Spoils* (1961) is a definitive study of the civil-service-reform movement from 1865 through the passage of the Pendleton Act in 1883.

The men who helped shape the Pendleton Act and who later became Mugwumps are discussed in *The Age of Reform* (1965) by Richard Hofstadter, which compares the Independent Republicans to other reformers at the turn of the century. John G. Sproat's *The Best-Men: Liberal Reformers in the Gilded Age* (1968) outlines the careers of several prominent Independents. Chapter 2 of Geoffrey T. Blodgett's *The Gentle Reformers: Massachusetts Democrats in the Cleveland Era* (1966) provides a portrait of Independent Republicans in the Bay State. Two articles specifically on the Mugwumps are Gordon S. Wood's "The Massachusetts Mugwumps," *New England Quarterly,* 33 (Dec., 1960), 435–51, and Gerald W. McFarland's "The New York Mugwumps of 1884: A Profile," *Political Science Quarterly,* 78 (March, 1963), 49–58.

Studies of the leaders of the Mugwump bolt include a nostalgic work by Edward Cary, *George William Curtis* (1895), and the more objective *George William Curtis and the Genteel Tradition* (1956) by Gordon Milne. Two creditable biographies of the chief Mugwump campaigner are Joseph Schafer's *Carl Schurz: Militant Liberal* (1930) and Claude Moore Fuess' *Carl Schurz: Reformer, 1829–1906* (1932). Fuess provides additional information about Schurz in "Carl Schurz, Henry Cabot Lodge and the Campaign of 1884," *New England Quarterly,* 5 (July, 1932), 453–82. Schurz's important writings are collected in *Speeches, Correspondence and Political Papers of Carl Schurz* (1913), Frederic Bancroft, ed.

A less influential Mugwump, Thomas Wentworth Higginson, described his life in *Cheerful Yesterdays* (1898). Having fought the Mugwump battle almost alone in Indiana, William Dudley Foulke recalled his struggles in *Fighting the Spoilsmen: Reminiscences of the Civil Service Reform Movement* (1919). Lyman Beecher Stowe wrote about his ancestor, Henry Ward Beecher, in *Saints, Sinners and Beechers* (1934), and Mark A. De Wolfe Howe told the story of a leading Massachusetts Mugwump in *Portrait of an Independent: Moorfield Storey* (1932). No Mugwump publicist did more for the movement than cartoonist Thomas Nast, and two historians have collected his drawings and briefly described his career: Albert Bigelow Paine in *Th. Nast: His Period and His Pictures* (1904) and John C. Vinson in *Thomas Nast: Political Cartoonist* (1967).

The most famous of the Independents who chose not to rebel, Theodore Roosevelt, recalled his dilemma in 1884 in *An Autobiography* (1913), as did Henry F. Pringle in *Theodore Roosevelt: A Biography* (1931). Additional information is available in Elting E. Morison's *The Letters of Theodore Roosevelt,* 8 vols. (1951–54), and James C. Malin's "Roosevelt and the Elections of 1884 and 1888," *Mississippi Valley Historical Review,* 14 (June, 1927), 25–46. The relationship between Roosevelt and his Massachusetts friend is spelled out in *Selections from the Correspondence of Theodore Roosevelt and Henry Cabot Lodge, 1884–1918,* 2 vols. (1925), and in Karl Schriftgieser's

The Gentleman from Massachusetts: Henry Cabot Lodge (1944). George F. Hoar handled his own defense in his *Autobiography of Seventy Years* (1906).

A look at the *Republican National Convention Official Proceedings* (1884) is essential for an understanding of the reformers' tactics. The controversial politician nominated at that convention had two stout defenders. Mary Abigail Dodge lived with the Blaine family for years and wrote a somewhat slanted *Biography of James G. Blaine* (1895), under the pseudonym Gail Hamilton. Another close friend and adviser, Edward Stanwood, produced a slightly more objective account in *James Gillespie Blaine* (1905). Not until almost a half century after the election did two less biased works appear: Charles Edward Russell's *Blaine of Maine, His Life and Times* (1931) and the definitive work by David Saville Muzzey, *James G. Blaine: A Political Idol of Other Days* (1934).

Blaine's opposition recorded its activities in the *Official Proceedings of the National Democratic Convention, 1884*. The Democratic candidate helped make the career of Allan Nevins, who wrote the excellent *Grover Cleveland: A Study in Courage* (1934) and selected and edited *Letters of Grover Cleveland* (1933). Two earlier biographies suffered from an oversympathetic view of the President: Robert McElroy, *Grover Cleveland: The Man and the Statesman* (1923) and Dennis Tilden Lynch, *Grover Cleveland: A Man Foursquare* (1932). For Cleveland's career as President, Horace Samuel Merrill's *Bourbon Leader: Grover Cleveland and the Democratic Party* (1957) is quite good. Two other books on the 1884 victor deserving mention are DeAlva Stanwood Alexander's *Four Famous New Yorkers: The Political Careers of Cleveland, Platt, Hill and Roosevelt* (1923) and William C. Hudson's *Random Recollections of an Old Political Reporter* (1911), written by a newspaperman closely associated with the Cleveland campaign.

Some of the most entertaining reading on the period appears in Benjamin F. Butler's *Butler's Book* (1892), a memoir that pulls no punches. Other views of the volatile Greenback candidate appear in Robert S. Holzman's *Stormy Ben Butler* (1954) and Hans L. Trefousse's *Ben Butler: The South Called Him BEAST!* (1957). Several other participants in the campaign have also become subjects of biographies. George Frederick Howe's *Chester A. Arthur: A Quarter Century of Machine Politics* (1934) has the same objectivity one finds in Nevins or Muzzey. The only lengthy study of Blaine's bitterest Republican enemy has been written by Donald Barr Chidsey, *The Gentleman from New York: A Life of Roscoe Conkling* (1935). The second volume of Royal Cortissoz' *The Life of Whitelaw Reid*, 2 vols. (1921), details the cooperation between Blaine and the vitriolic editor. Democratic leaders' careers are described in Alexander Clarence Flick's *Samuel Jones Tilden: A Study in Political Sagacity* (1939); James A. Barnes' *John G. Carlisle: Financial Statesman* (1931); and Mark D. Hirsch's *William C. Whitney: Modern Warwick* (1948). Whitney rounded up financial backing for the campaign that Maryland Senator Gorman ran for Cleveland, as described in John R. Lambert's *Arthur Pue Gorman* (1953).

Dealing primarily with the election's aftermath is Herbert Croly's *Marcus Alonzo Hanna* (1912), a biography of the Republican leader who pulled the party together for 1896. Harry Thurston Peck's *Twenty Years of the Republic 1885–1905* (1906) makes delightful reading even today. Finally, Paul W. Glad's *McKinley, Bryan, and the People* (1964) picks up the story where this study ends.

Index